Why It's OK

to Ignore Politics

Do you feel like you're the only person at your office without an "I Voted!" sticker on Election Day? It turns out that you're far from alone—100 million eligible U.S. voters never went to the polls in 2016. That's about 35 million more than voted for the winning presidential candidate.

In this book, Christopher Freiman explains why these 100 million need not feel guilty. *Why It's OK to Ignore Politics* argues that you're under no obligation to be politically active. Freiman addresses new objections to political abstention as well as some old chestnuts ("But what if *everyone* stopped voting?"). He also synthesizes recent empirical work showing how our political motivations distort our choices and reasoning. Because participating in politics is not an effective way to do good, Freiman argues that we actually have a moral duty to *disengage* from politics and instead take direct action to make the world a better place.

Key Features

- Makes the case against a duty of political participation for a nonexpert audience
- Presupposes no knowledge of philosophy or political science and is written in a style free of technical jargon

- Addresses the standard, much-repeated arguments for why one should vote (e.g., one shouldn't free ride on the efforts of others)
- Presents the growing literature on politically motivated reasoning in an accessible and entertaining way
- Covers a significant amount of new ground in the debate over a duty of political participation (e.g., whether participating absolves us of our complicity in state injustice)
- Challenges the increasingly popular argument from philosophers and economists that swing state voting is effective altruism
- Discusses the therapeutic benefits of ignoring politics— it's good for you, your relationships, and society as a whole

Christopher Freiman is Associate Professor of Philosophy at William & Mary. He is the author of *Unequivocal Justice* (2017).

Why It's OK: The Ethics and Aesthetics of How We Live

Philosophers often build cogent arguments for unpopular positions. Recent examples include cases against marriage and pregnancy, for treating animals as our equals, and dismissing some popular art as aesthetically inferior. What philosophers have done less often is to offer compelling arguments for widespread and established human behavior, like getting married, having children, eating animals, and going to the movies. But if one role for philosophy is to help us reflect on our lives and build sound justifications for our beliefs and actions, it seems odd that philosophers would neglect arguments for the lifestyles most people—including many philosophers—actually lead. Unfortunately, philosophers' inattention to normalcy has meant that the ways of life that define our modern societies have gone largely without defense, even as whole literatures have emerged to condemn them.

Why It's OK: The Ethics and Aesthetics of How We Live seeks to remedy that. It's a series of books that provides accessible, sound, and often new and creative arguments for widespread ethical and aesthetic values. Made up of short volumes that assume no previous knowledge of philosophy from the reader, the series recognizes that philosophy is just as important for understanding what we already believe as it is for criticizing the status quo. The series isn't meant to make us complacent about what we value; rather, it helps and challenges us to think more deeply about the values that give our daily lives meaning.

Titles in Series:

For further information about this series, please visit: www.routledge.com/Why-Its-OK/book-series/WIOK

Why It's OK to Ignore Politics

CHRISTOPHER FREIMAN

Why It's OK
to Ignore Politics

Routledge
Taylor & Francis Group

NEW YORK AND LONDON

First published 2021
by Routledge
52 Vanderbilt Avenue, New York, NY 10017

and by Routledge
2 Park Square, Milton Park, Abingdon, Oxon, OX14 4RN

*Routledge is an imprint of the Taylor & Francis Group, an informa
business*

Library of Congress Cataloging-in-Publication Data
A catalog record for this book has been requested

ISBN: 978-1-138-38899-4 (hbk)
ISBN: 978-1-138-38900-7 (pbk)
ISBN: 978-1-003-03965-5 (ebk)

Typeset in Joanna MT Pro and DIN pro
by Apex CoVantage, LLC

To Mary,
for making my life immeasurably better

Contents

Contents

To get a sense of just how strongly people feel about political participation, consider the case of San Francisco 49ers quarterback Colin Kaepernick. Kaepernick, who became famous for kneeling in protest during the national anthem, didn't vote in the 2016 presidential election. Even though Kaepernick donated one million dollars of his salary and all of the proceeds from his jersey sales to charity, he was admonished in the pages of *Forbes* on the grounds that his "failure to vote tarnishes his credibility as a social activist."[6] Kaepernick's donations and volunteering efforts apparently only take his "message so far. In order to enact long-lasting social change, he must take part in the democratic process."[7]

The notion that Kaepernick's charitable work fails to offset his refusal to vote reveals a fascinating belief about the moral weight of political participation. There was only a one in a billion chance that Kaepernick's vote would have made a difference to the outcome of the presidential election.[8] So his (uncast) vote was worth next to nothing, while his donations were worth over a million dollars—and he still got bashed for not voting!

Not only do the media and our fellow citizens urge us to dive into the democratic process, moral and political authorities do it too. Political philosophers have long extolled the virtues of democratic participation.[9] Pope Paul VI declared that "all citizens" have "the duty to use their free vote to further the common good."[10] According to U.S. Citizenship and Immigration Services, one of the responsibilities of American citizens is to "participate in the democratic process."[11] Even children's televisions shows implore us to roll up our sleeves, do our civic duty, and get politically active; I've been bombarded with pro-participation messages while watching *Sesame Street* ("Big Bird, it is *very* important that everybody vote!") and *Daniel Tiger's*

Neighborhood with my kids. When John Stuart Mill, the Pope, and *Sesame Street* all line up on the same side of an argument, you'd better take it seriously.

Yet despite the widespread belief in the moral importance of participating in politics, many Americans simply don't do it. Roughly 100 million eligible voters declined to cast a ballot in the 2016 U.S. presidential election.[12] Think of it this way: if "not voting" had been a candidate, it would have won by a landslide. (Political philosophers don't vote at higher rates than other professors, for what it's worth.)[13] Rates of participation in political activities other than voting are even lower.[14]

This book argues that there's nothing wrong with ignoring politics. To the contrary: you should disengage from politics to pursue more effective forms of altruism. Instead of watching presidential debates, attending city council meetings, and writing letters to your representative, you should spend your time on charitable activities that are more likely to change people's lives for the better. Go ahead: be apolitical, guilt free.

Here's how I make my case. I begin by arguing that a general moral duty to participate cannot be grounded in the good consequences of your participation. To start, it's deceptively hard to know whether one's participation is aimed at good consequences rather than bad ones. In Chapter 1, I show that figuring out which policies and politicians to support takes more information than you probably think. It's no surprise that you need to know about the candidates and their platforms, but you'll also need to research their track records instead of relying on their campaign promises. Next, you'll want to brush up on the details of the legislation they've supported. And to competently evaluate the legislation, you'll need knowledge of political science, economics, environmental science, and moral philosophy. Since most of us lack this knowledge, we can't be confident that our political participation is aimed at outcomes that will help rather than hurt society. We're like doctors prescribing a medication we've never researched. (Many of us haven't even read the label.)

Next, you need to use the information you acquire to arrive at accurate political beliefs. But Chapter 2 argues that accuracy tends not to be our aim when we reason about politics. We're vulnerable to *politically motivated reasoning*: the (unconscious) goal of our political deliberation is not to find the truth but rather to protect our identity as a loyal member of our political "team"—Democrat, Republican, libertarian, socialist, and so on. We are distressingly good at dismissing, downgrading, and explaining away evidence that indicates we're on the wrong side of the political aisle.

Politically motivated reasoners shouldn't trust themselves to evaluate political information properly. If, for instance, you know that you'll selectively accept information that affirms your belief that Republicans are better than Democrats and selectively dismiss information that tells you otherwise, then you should be skeptical of your belief that the Republicans really *are* better. In the event that the Democrats are better, you'd never know it.

Not only do you have reason to doubt that your participation is aimed at good consequences rather than bad ones, you also have reason to doubt that your political activism will have a meaningful impact. As I discuss in Chapter 3, almost all of the political action you might take to advance your cause is going to be ineffective. Your campaign donation, your protest sign, and your Facebook post won't change large-scale political outcomes. Even if you live in a key swing state where there is a nontrivial chance that your vote will make a difference, voting remains a dubious bet because it's exceedingly hard to know whether your vote is cast for a candidate who will make society better rather than worse.

Furthermore, resources channeled into political engagement are resources that could be spent on causes that have a higher expected social benefit. Time spent watching C-SPAN and waiting in line at the polls is time not spent volunteering at a soup kitchen. Money donated to a political campaign is money not donated to save the lives of children in Ghana who would otherwise die from malaria. Thus, insofar as we care about making the lives of others better, we ought to ignore politics and focus on effective altruism instead.

Chapter 4 asks whether political abstention is wrong because it involves "free riding" on the political contributions made by others. Perhaps it's unfair that I benefit from the time and effort my fellow citizens spend working for good governance without reciprocating with political participation of my own. In reply, I defend a division of labor: it's inefficient for all citizens to dedicate themselves to politics just as it's inefficient for all citizens to dedicate themselves to pizza delivery. You can repay your debt to politically active citizens by contributing to society in nonpolitical ways just as you can repay your debt to a delivery driver with a tip instead of delivering a pizza to her house. Indeed, you can typically contribute to the very same ends as politically active citizens—feeding the hungry, sheltering the homeless, enriching the poor, and so on—more effectively by taking direct, nonpolitical action.

In Chapter 5 I consider the suggestion that we must be politically engaged, not to compensate our fellow citizens for the good political work they've done, but rather to resist the injustices that our government perpetuates in our name. The problem with this argument is that any individual's effort to reform their government is unlikely to change things for the better. For this reason, it is preferable to undertake direct action to make the victims of injustice whole rather than attempt to bring about systemic reform. If you've received stolen goods and cannot bring the thief to justice, you should prioritize returning those goods to their rightful owner.

Maybe the duty of political participation lies in the message participation sends. When you vote for better schools, you express your commitment to educating children even if your single vote doesn't result in better schools. And messages matter—you wouldn't spit on a loved one's grave, would you? Chapter 6 explains why this style of argument is unconvincing. The best expression of concern for justice and the common good is nonpolitical action that effectively promotes justice and the common good. If anything, engaging in purely expressive political activity sends a *bad* message. By analogy, mailing your injured friend a "Get Well Soon" letter instead of getting her urgent medical care indicates that you aren't *really* that committed to her health. To appropriately express concern for a problem, take action that helps fix the problem.

Chapter 7 explores the therapeutic benefits of ignoring politics. Political philosophers often argue that political engagement is central to a well-lived life and a well-run society. And that's understandable—engaging with politics is their job, after all.[15]

We tend to think that activities that occupy us ought to occupy others. Here's a more-or-less accurate recap of a conversation I once had with my dentist:

Her: You're coming in for a cleaning every six months, right?
Me: I am.
Her: And you're brushing twice a day?

Me: Yep.

Her: With an electric toothbrush using soft bristles?

Me: That's right.

Her: Do you use a pre-brushing mouthwash to loosen plaque?

Me: Uh-huh.

Her: What about flossing? Do you floss at least once a day?

Me: I do.

Her: After brushing, do you use a fluoride rinse?

Me: Religiously.

Her: Good. And what about a Waterpik?

Me: No, I don't use a Waterpik.

Her: [*Audibly sucking in air through her teeth*] Ooooh, you *really* should use a Waterpik.

Me: [*Sits silently in shame*]

While I appreciate her dedication to her craft, I have a life to live. I can't quit my job to optimize my oral hygiene regimen. That dentistry is the center of my dentist's universe is no surprise, but that doesn't mean that my life needs to revolve around my teeth. (I've since coined the *Waterpik Fallacy* and found it applicable to virtually all areas of my life—keep an eye out for it and I'm sure you will too.) Similarly, I understand why some political philosophers argue that political engagement is necessary for a person to flourish, but an apolitical life need not be an impoverished one. In fact, it turns out that as partisan politics consumes more of our lives, we become less happy, less trusting, and less understanding of others. It can even make people believe that the death of their political opponents would be a good thing. Needless to say, this situation is not a healthy one. So you should *deemphasize* the role of politics in your life—your well-being, your relationships, and society as a whole will be better for it.

I close the book in the Conclusion by taking my previous arguments a step further. Not only is there no moral duty to participate in politics, political participation tends to be *morally wrong*. As noted, the resources you invest in unhelpful political activity are resources that could be invested in effective charities that combat poverty, blindness, malaria, and more. I defend the claim that it is wrong to perform an action that is significantly and needlessly worse than another action you could perform—for instance, it would be wrong to give your bottle of water to the stranger who simply wants to slick back his hair rather than the one dying of thirst. I conclude that it's wrong to give your time to political engagement when you could literally save lives instead.

One

> I am wiser than this man; it is likely that neither of us knows anything worthwhile, but he thinks he knows something when he does not, whereas when I do not know, neither do I think I know; so I am likely to be wiser than he to this small extent, that I do not think I know when I do not know.
>
> —Socrates in Plato's *Apology* 21d

If you want to do good in politics, you first need to *know* what's good in politics. Will minimum wage legislation increase unemployment? Is entitlement spending unsustainable? Should college debt be forgiven? Is taxation theft? Is abortion murder?

You shouldn't participate in politics if you have little reason to think that your favored policies and politicians are more likely to do good than harm. Just as a doctor shouldn't prescribe a medication if she doesn't know whether it will help or hurt her patient, you shouldn't vote or protest if you don't know whether your political causes will help or hurt society.[1]

Figuring out which politicians and policies to support takes more work than you probably think. First, you need information that most people don't have. What are the candidates' platforms? What does the text of their sponsored legislation say? Next, you need to *evaluate* the information that you've got.

Is the legislation efficient? To answer this question, you'll need to learn basic economics. Is the legislation fair? Now you've got to crack open some books on moral and political philosophy. And once you've finished analyzing this policy, you've got to do the same for the others.

In this chapter, I argue that you shouldn't have much, if any, confidence in your political judgment. Few of us know the specifics of the policies at stake in political debates; even fewer of us know the social science and philosophy needed to competently evaluate them. In brief, most of us don't know what we need to know to determine whether our political causes would do good or do harm.

INFORMATION ABOUT PARTICULARS

To illustrate the challenge facing political participants, let's run with the medication analogy. When a doctor is deciding whether or not to prescribe a drug, she should ask herself the following questions. What's in the drug? What does it actually do? In light of the risks and rewards, should I prescribe it to my patient?

Similarly, to determine whether you should canvass for a particular candidate, you need to ask yourself a series of questions. What is the candidate's policy platform? What legislation did she *actually* support (as opposed to what she says in her campaign speeches)? What did that legislation *actually* say? What did that legislation actually *do*? And were the effects good or bad?

Researching a candidate's policy platform is easy enough—a quick Google search will do the trick. Suppose, according to her website, Candidate Candice supports stricter pollution laws and touts investments in public infrastructure. So far, so good.

Now you know what the candidate says. But what does she *do*? You can't simply read her website, dust off your hands, and declare your job done. Has Candice really supported stricter pollution laws in the past?

To get a more accurate picture of Candice's performance, you can start by taking a peek at her voting record. But even that's not enough. Suppose Candice voted for the "Pollution Reduction Act." That sounds nice, but what's in the Pollution Reduction Act? To answer this question, you'll probably need to pull up the text of the Pollution Reduction Act and start reading. Did it institute a carbon tax, a cap-and-trade system, solar subsidies, or a toothless policy with cosmetic reforms but no substance?

At this point you've got a handle on Candice's record on pollution: she supports a cap-and-trade system. Now you're getting somewhere. But wait—what exactly is a cap-and-trade system? This may seem like a frivolous question, but it isn't: nearly twice as many Americans think that cap-and-trade is about regulating Wall Street or health care than environmental policy.[2]

There's more. If Candice keeps fighting for cap-and-trade, will other legislators cooperate? If something does get passed, will it be enervated by loopholes favored by special interests? And how much of a difference will domestic environmental reform make on the global scale—the scale needed to genuinely address climate change?

If you're like the typical American, you don't know the answers to these questions. As political scientist Larry Bartels puts it, "The political ignorance of the American voter is one of the best-documented features of contemporary politics."[3] Or, in the words of political scientist Robert Luskin, most of us "know jaw-droppingly little about politics."[4]

Roughly one-third of surveyed Americans possess virtually no political knowledge.[5] The average respondent answered less than half of the questions about basic political knowledge (e.g., whether federal spending on the poor had decreased in the recent past) correctly.[6] Given that the test was multiple choice, the typical respondent only fared moderately better than a random guesser.[7]

Only 42% of Americans can name the three branches of government.[8] Seventy percent don't know who both of their state senators are.[9] Only about a quarter of Americans can name the Chief Justice of the Supreme Court.[10] When asked to identify just one candidate for the House of Representatives in their own district, only 15% of people could.[11] When asked to identify two candidates, only 4% could.[12]

And get a load of this: 40% of Americans cannot name a single right that the First Amendment protects; significantly more Americans think that the First Amendment protects the right to bear arms than know all of the freedoms it actually protects.[13] Forty-two percent of American adults think that Marx's principle "from each according to his ability, to each according to his needs" is from the founding documents of the United States.[14]

Or consider foreign aid. On average, Americans believe that 25% of the federal budget goes to foreign aid. The correct answer? About 1%—an answer that only 1 in 20 Americans know. Before learning the right figures, most Americans believe that the federal government spends too much on foreign aid—after being corrected, that number is cut in half.[15]

I could go on, but you get the point.[16] If you're like the typical American, you should do more homework before you pass judgment on the country's foreign aid policy. To judge whether America is spending too much or too little on foreign aid, you first need to know how much America is actually spending on foreign aid. Ninety-five percent of us don't know that. And we're not just off by a hair or two—we think that spending is 25 times greater than it is.

SOCIAL SCIENCE

Next you need to evaluate the information you acquire. You might know the *quantity* of federal spending on foreign aid, but what about the *quality*? Is government aid to foreign countries working well? Could it be better spent? Just as competent doctors use medical knowledge to assess a drug's ingredients and what effect they are likely to have on your body, competent political participants use social scientific knowledge to assess policies and their likely effects on the country and the world.

Here again, if you're like the typical American, you probably lack this knowledge. By way of example, consider the Scared Straight program that arranges confrontations between convicted criminals and youth found guilty of misdemeanors in the interest of "scaring" the youth off the path of crime. It turns out that Scared Straight dramatically *increases* the odds of young people committing a crime.[17] One study found that the program did over $200 worth of harm for every dollar spent.[18] But only 15% of people quizzed on the program knew that it increased crime.[19]

People's knowledge of the effectiveness of social programs in general is lacking. Consider experimental subjects who were tested on their knowledge of the efficacy of ten programs (including Scared Straight) that were well researched, easy to understand, and yielded clear conclusions.[20] They performed only slightly better than random chance (and participants who didn't even bother to read the program descriptions actually outperformed those who did).

The public is dramatically uninformed about social science generally. For instance, the economist Bryan Caplan has shown that most of us hold systematically biased beliefs about core economic issues.[21] Overall, there is a large gap between the economic beliefs of lay people and the beliefs of expert economists.[22] We also see a disconnect between the beliefs of the public and the beliefs of political and scientific experts.[23]

You can test your own understanding of a central economic problem right now: what is the overall rise in national income within the next 25 years if the economy grows at an annual rate of 5%? When given this question, 92% of respondents underestimated the number.[24] The correct answer is 238.64%; the average estimate was 82.76%.[25]

But so what? Maybe a given economic policy will shave half a percentage point from the growth rate. No big deal, right? Wrong. Nobel Prize-winning economist Paul Romer explains why small differences in the growth rate can have monumental impacts over time:

> In the modern version of an old legend, an investment banker asks to be paid by placing one penny on the first square of a chess board, two pennies on the second square, four on the third, etc. If the banker had asked that only the white squares be used, the initial penny would double in value thirty-one times, leaving $21.5 million on the last square. Using both the black and the white squares makes the penny grow to $92,000,000 billion. People are reasonably good at forming estimates based on addition, but for operations such as compounding that depend on repeated multiplication, we systematically underestimate

how fast things grow. As a result we often lose sight of how important the average rate of growth is for an economy. . . . For a nation the choices that determine whether income doubles with every generation, or instead with every other generation, dwarf all other policy concerns.[26]

Slight changes in the economic growth rate are probably political afterthoughts for most of us. But this could be a grave mistake.[27]

THE ILLUSION OF EXPLANATORY DEPTH

Perhaps you're tempted to count yourself an exception to the general rule of American political ignorance. And maybe you are. But it's worth noting that those with low political knowledge tend to be overconfident in their political knowledge.[28]

We're also vulnerable to the "illusion of explanatory depth"—we think we understand the world better than we actually do. In a study conducted by Leonid Rozenblit and Frank Keil, subjects were asked to rate their understanding of artifacts like zippers and flush toilets.[29] Then they were asked to write step-by-step explanations of how these things work. It turns out that subjects initially overrated their understanding of the objects to a dramatic extent; their self-assessed ratings of their understanding plummeted after confronting their failures to explain the mechanics of the objects. As Rozenblit and Keil put it, "People feel they understand complex phenomena with far greater precision, coherence, and depth than they really do."[30]

Another study found a similar result for political beliefs.[31] Subjects were asked how well they understood various policy issues like single-payer health care and cap-and-trade. They were then asked to give a mechanistic explanation of how one of the policies worked. Subjects reported a far weaker understanding of the issue after their attempt at an explanation.

A zipper is a simple system. It has few parts and they fit together in a fairly straightforward way. You can *see* a zipper. You've used one thousands of times. And still most of us don't understand how it works.

A socio-political system is, needless to say, more complicated than a zipper. It has billions of parts (many of which are conscious, hard-to-predict agents like you and me) that interact with each other in unanticipated ways. Unlike a zipper, it wasn't deliberately designed; rather, it's the by-product of countless people acting out their own plans without an eye toward the bigger picture.[32]

Because it's hard to understand how society works, it's hard to predict how new policies will change how it works. Predicting the far-flung effects of even straightforward-seeming laws is notoriously difficult. General social scientific knowledge won't be enough.

The "Cobra Effect" illustrates this point.[33] The colonial government in Delhi was worried about the growing number of venomous cobras in the city, so it offered a bounty on cobra skins to reduce the population. However, it turns out that the bounty paid for a cobra skin was more than the cost of farming a cobra. Consequently, many began farming cobras simply to collect the bounty. When the government learned of this response, it repealed the bounty. The farmed cobras were subsequently released into the city—dramatically increasing the total cobra population. The bounty was not simply ineffective; it was downright counterproductive.

Something similar happened when Mexico City banned the use of each particular car on a specified day of the week to reduce pollution and congestion. Drivers responded by buying additional cars to receive additional driving permits. The ultimate result was an *increase* in driving.[34]

It might seem easy to diagnose what went wrong in these cases in hindsight. But it's much harder to accurately predict the future. Even experts tend to have poor predictive track records.[35] Most famously, Philip Tetlock studied the predictions of 284 experts on matters like the economy and elections over the course of 20 years.[36] The conclusion, as summarized by Louis Menand, is that in many cases "human beings who spend their lives studying the state of the world . . . are poorer forecasters than dart-throwing monkeys."[37]

To get a sense of how hard it is to predict job performance for, say, a U.S. president, consider how hard it is to predict the performance for a simpler job: quarterback of a football team. Talent evaluators in the National Football League have spent their entire adult lives studying game film. They interview prospective quarterbacks. They interview their college coaches, their friends, and their family. They subject the prospects to psychological evaluations and intelligence tests. They study how fast the prospects run, how high they can jump, and how much weight they can lift. They hire private investigators to follow them in their leisure time. They recruit MIT graduates to crunch the prospects' statistics. They may even scrutinize how the prospects pour ketchup—it's apparently critical to check whether a football player taps the "57" on the Heinz bottle for maximum ketchup-dispensing efficiency.[38] Moreover, millions of dollars and careers hang in the balance. And guess what: professional talent evaluators are still awful at predicting the future performance of quarterbacks.[39]

A quarterback also has a comparatively simple job. He's only in charge of ten other people on the field and has clearly defined standards of success and failure. By contrast, presidents have an extraordinarily complicated job with highly contested standards of success. They answer to millions of citizens and employees with trillions of dollars and international consequences at stake. If evaluators with all of the incentive, resources, and expertise in the world can't accurately predict football performance, what hope is there for us to predict presidential performance?

You might feel confident that a given presidential candidate will change things for the better, but remember: "People feel they understand complex phenomena with far greater precision, coherence, and depth than they really do."[40] As philosopher Michael Huemer says,

> Society is a complex mechanism whose repair, if possible at all, would require a precise and detailed understanding of a kind that no one today possesses. Unsatisfying as it may seem, the wisest course for political agents is often simply to stop trying to solve society's problems.[41]

If you don't know how to fix a zipper, you probably don't know how to fix society.

CAN WE TAKE A SHORTCUT?

One common objection to the argument that the average citizen is insufficiently informed to make wise political decisions alleges that shortcuts are available, thus enabling citizens to forgo their own detailed research.[42] Maybe you've let your subscription to The Economist lapse and have fallen behind on current events, but no worries, you can just glance at the candidate they endorse and vote for her. The cognitive shortcuts or "heuristics" you might use include following the advice of social scientific experts, the candidates' parties, candidate endorsements, and more. By analogy, I don't need to scour medical journals to determine whether I should take a particular pharmaceutical—I just ask my doctor.

Of course, a shortcut won't help if it's a bad one. (Asking "anti-vaxx" Facebook groups whether vaccines cause autism is a shortcut you might use to bypass the medical journals, but it won't lead you to true beliefs about vaccines.) For instance, Samuel Popkin suggests that voters may consider whether candidates show "familiarity with a voter's culture," which can reveal the extent to which candidates relate to and care about them.[43] But as political scientists Christopher Achen and Larry Bartels note, it is difficult to distinguish reliable cues from unreliable ones.[44] By way of example, in 2003, presidential candidate John Kerry had the unmitigated gall to order a Philly cheesesteak with Swiss cheese (!) instead of the customary (and, let's face it, correct) topping—Cheez Whiz.[45] To make matters worse, Kerry nibbled on the cheesesteak instead of eating it "the proper way," namely "throwing fistfuls of steak into the gaping maw, fingers dripping."[46] This debacle apparently caused some observers to regard Kerry as an out of touch snob.[47] Now, as strenuously as I object to Kerry's cheese selection, I must admit that cheese selection is a silly shortcut to use to judge a presidential candidate.

You might take your job as a political participant more seriously than that. Perhaps your political opinions are based less on cheesesteak etiquette and more on expert judgment. Let's set aside worries about the accuracy of expert judgment for a moment. Even if there are reliable political experts out there, will you make use of them?[48] A further obstacle for those who would use shortcuts remains: our perception of who counts as an expert is warped by partisan bias.[49] Think about it: anti-vaxxers don't regard their doctor as an expert on the topic of vaccines. She's a shill for Big Pharma. Marxists don't think that Harvard economist Greg Mankiw is an expert on economics. He's a neoliberal ideologue. The availability of informed opinion isn't helpful if we seek out ideologically friendly experts to confirm the (uninformed) opinion we started with—and this is exactly what we tend to do.[50]

A similar problem arises for the claim that we can use parties, endorsements, and professional pundits as proxies for our own views. George Will is a fine stand-in if you're a staunch conservative. But the most important question remains unanswered: is staunch conservativism true? By analogy, few would advance the following claim: "You don't need to do all that work figuring out what to think about religion. Don't bother reading the world's major religious texts or analyzing the theological claims they make—just use the Pope as a proxy." No doubt the Pope is a good proxy if you want to know what a Catholic should think about contraception. But the question of whether you should be a Catholic in the first place is still unsettled.

As a summing up point, I'll note that analyses show that informed citizens and uninformed citizens have very different policy preferences and cast very different votes.[51] So whether uninformed citizens are not making use of the shortcuts available to them or simply not using them well, the fact remains that shortcuts tend not to function as effective substitutes for intensive political education. (If you decide that you'll study hard to figure out which experts to trust as stand-ins, then you at least somewhat defeat the purpose of looking for a shortcut.)[52]

Before moving on, I'll note that it is easier to acquire relevant knowledge at the level of local politics than national or global politics. *Easier*—but not easy. My city recently imposed a sales tax to fund tourism. This policy raises a number of questions. For instance, should the city impose a sales tax at all? That's going to involve redistributing income away from some people and toward others. Is this fair? Is this efficient? Why think that the Tourism Council will put that money to better use than taxpayers would? Supposing the tax is a good idea, how high should it be? And which specific projects should the tax revenue fund? An aquatics center? A sports complex? Music festivals? I haven't the slightest idea. So even though acquiring information about local politics (or, say, a single national political issue) is more manageable than brushing up on dozens of large-scale political problems, let's not underestimate the commitment it takes.

MORAL QUESTIONS

Suppose, for the sake of argument, that you buy a crystal ball that enables you to predict all of the effects of the policies of the competing candidates in perfect detail. You know, for instance, that a proposal to ease U.S. immigration restrictions will raise the income of the immigrants and the average American but will lower the incomes of the lowest-wage American workers. To aim your participation at the right immigration policy, you need to know whether that's a trade-off that we *should* make.

Or imagine that you acquire conclusive evidence that the death penalty deters murder but will sometimes result in the execution of innocent people. Should we implement it? Is the state justified in instituting a policy that will reduce innocent deaths on net, foreseeing that the policy will nevertheless kill some innocent people in the process? Do we want the state in the business of killing its citizens? Does the punishment of death fit the crime of murder?

Social science can't answer these questions. Social science attempts to tell you what is or what will be, but it can't tell you what should be. Figuring out how to weigh the interests of citizens and foreigners or determining what counts as just punishment are jobs for philosophy. The list of moral questions embedded within our policy debates is long: is abortion morally equivalent to infanticide? Should nonhuman animals have legal rights? Are richer nations obliged to send foreign aid to poorer nations? When is humanitarian military intervention warranted? Does the right to self-defense imply a right to own a gun? Cigarette smoking is unhealthy, but might you have the right to make unhealthy decisions for yourself?

The philosophical dimensions of public policy raise new problems because it's exceedingly difficult to have confidence in one's answers to philosophical questions. I'll put it this way: philosophers will tell you that it's hard to figure out what makes a chair a chair, so it's safe to assume that it's hard to figure out the right way to govern a 300-million-person nation state.

Most of us are unacquainted with any of the enormous literature on the relevant topics. To take just one example: in the last 40 years or so, roughly 800 papers on abortion have appeared in major philosophy journals.[53] I'd wager that the typical American citizen has read zero of these articles. If you've taken some philosophy classes, I'd bump that number up to two. So odds are that you've read, at most, one-quarter of one percent of the professional moral analysis of abortion. This is hardly enough reading to justify a confident opinion on a deeply contested issue. Now rinse and repeat for other controversial moral and political problems: gun ownership, income redistribution, immigration, military intervention, drug policy, and so on. It's likely that most of us haven't done our homework.

In brief, you need to do a daunting amount of research to make competent political decisions. Since you probably haven't done enough, here's my recommendation: recognize, as Socrates did, that wisdom often consists in simply knowing what we do not know. And if we know that we don't know the right way to govern the country, we have a powerful reason to either abstain from politics or make a dedicated effort to learn what we need to learn. In what follows, I'll explain why making such an effort is likely not worth your while.

Two

smbc-comics.com

Perhaps you've already acquired plenty of political information. You know who your representative is. You've aced Economics 101. You listen to philosophy podcasts. Still, your job isn't done. To arrive at accurate political beliefs, you not only need information—you need to make good use of it.

Ideally, a political participant would clinically survey the empirical evidence and philosophical arguments and dutifully follow them wherever they lead. They'd be like a juror who enters the courtroom without any preconceived notions of the defendant's guilt or innocence, no personal stake in the case, and ready to weigh the evidence without bias. The juror's only motivation is to arrive at the truth.

Unfortunately, most of us aren't like this. We're more like an observer hearing a case in which his mother is on trial for murder. This observer would no doubt be highly motivated to believe that his mother is not guilty. He'd enthusiastically accept evidence that exonerates her. And he'd be allergic to evidence that implicates her. The eyewitness who claims that she saw his mother harmlessly shopping at the grocery store at the time of the murder is credible; the eyewitness who testifies that he saw her fire the fatal shot is surely a liar.

Needless to say, you shouldn't trust this observer's judgment of his mother's guilt or innocence. The (unconscious) goal of his reasoning about the trial is not the truth but rather vindicating his mother. Now maybe his mother is innocent, but you shouldn't trust his judgment if you know he is in the grip of "motivated reasoning." Here the problem is not that the observer lacks information; rather, it's that he doesn't use the information to arrive at accurate beliefs.

The same goes for the way most of us process political information—we're vulnerable to politically motivated reasoning. The (unconscious) goal of our reasoning about politics is not to arrive at the truth but rather to protect our identity as a member of our partisan group (e.g., Democrats, Republicans, libertarians, socialists, and so on).[1] Political partisans are often analogized to sports fans: we care more about defending our team than getting at the truth.[2]

It turns out that the analogy between political partisans and sports fans is surprisingly apt. Evidence indicates that sports fans are far more likely to spot officiating errors when the errors harm their team instead of their rival.[3] Fans' loyalty to their team shapes how they interpret the events they see on the field.

Similarly, political partisans' loyalty to their side shapes how they interpret information. One study asked subjects to watch a video of a protest.[4] Half were told they were watching a protest of an abortion clinic; the other half were told they were watching a protest of the military's policy (at the time) of banning openly gay, lesbian, and bisexual Americans from service. Liberals' and conservatives' responses to both moral and empirical questions about the protests depended on whether the political cause of the protestors aligned with their own.

For instance, subjects were asked whether the police officers tasked with directing traffic and controlling the crowd near the protest violated the protestors' rights. Seventy percent of conservatives said that the police violated the rights of those protesting the abortion clinic compared to only 16% who said that the police violated the rights of those protesting the military recruitment center.[5] By contrast, 76% of liberals said that the police violated the rights of those protesting the military recruitment center compared to only 28% who said the same about the abortion protestors.[6]

What about comparatively straightforward matters? Only 39% of conservatives said that the abortion protesters were blocking pedestrians, but 74% said that the military protestors were.[7] Here again, we see the reverse result for liberals: 45% said that the military protesters were blocking pedestrians, with 76% saying that the abortion protestors were.[8]

Remember, subjects saw the same video. But they were motivated to form beliefs that put their own political team in a positive light and the opposing political team in a negative light. You can study politics until your head and eyes ache, but your acquisition of information won't help get you to the truth if your aim is aligning yourself with other members of your team rather than forming accurate beliefs.[9]

In this chapter, I'll review some of the empirical literature on politically motivated reasoning and investigate its philosophical implications. I'll argue that the chances are quite good that you are susceptible to politically motivated reasoning. Moreover, this susceptibility should further reduce your confidence in your own political beliefs. Just as you should doubt yourself when you think that your favorite football team is always on the correct side of disputed officiating calls, you should doubt yourself when you think that your own political team is always on the correct side of political debate. And be warned: the more politically knowledgeable you are, the more likely you are to fall prey to politically motivated reasoning.[10]

POLITICALLY MOTIVATED REASONING

There is substantial literature on the pervasiveness of politically motivated reasoning; I'll merely review some of the greatest hits. Consider a fascinating neuroscientific study that illustrates just how threatening we find information that challenges our political identity.[11] Participants were placed in a functional MRI scanner and asked to consider challenges to both their nonpolitical beliefs (e.g., whether Thomas Edison was the inventor of the lightbulb) and political beliefs (e.g., whether abortion ought to be legal). Researchers found that people were significantly more likely to change their nonpolitical beliefs than their political beliefs.[12]

But here's the most interesting result: subjects' brains reacted to threats to their political identity in roughly the same way that they would react to *physical* threats.[13] As one of the researchers, Sarah Gimbel, put it: "The response in the brain that we see is very similar to what would happen if, say, you were walking through the forest and came across a bear."[14] Think about that: learning that you might be wrong about politics causes the same sort of reaction as running into a bear in the woods. We're protective of our political selves just as we're protective of our physical selves.

It is little surprise, then, that people are willing to pay a monetary price to avoid interacting with viewpoints threatening to their political identity.[15] One study gave subjects the option of reading controversial political opinions with which they agreed for a chance at winning $7. Alternatively, they could read opinions with which they disagreed for a chance at $10. Roughly two-thirds of the subjects elected to read the friendly opinions, even though it meant losing the opportunity to win more money. (Republicans and Democrats were equally likely to avoid identity-threatening information.)

When we *do* confront identity-threatening information, we do our best to process it in a way that defuses the threat. Subjects presented with two (invented) studies on the deterrent effect of the death penalty rated the evidence as stronger when it supported their preexisting view on the death penalty and rated it as weaker when it undermined their view.[16] Liberals are more adept at spotting flaws in arguments supporting conservative conclusions; the reverse is true for conservatives.[17] Another study revealed that Democrats are better at finding inconsistencies in Republicans' statements than statements made by their fellow Democrats *and* at rationalizing away inconsistencies in Democrats' statements (again, the reverse is true for Republicans); moreover, fMRI results found that the subjects appeared to experience "reward or relief" after processing away the "threatening information."[18]

To be clear: it would be a mistake to think that partisans stick to their policy preferences through thick and thin. Rather, they are wedded to their political *identity*. Political scientists Christopher Achen and Larry Bartels observe that "group and partisan loyalties, not policy preferences or ideologies, are fundamental in democratic politics."[19] People tend to shift their political opinions in ways that are congenial to their partisan identity. We see this both in the laboratory and in the wild.

Psychologist Geoffrey Cohen discovered that a policy's party affiliation mattered more to partisans than the policy's content.[20] In Cohen's study, liberals and conservatives were presented with a characteristically liberal proposal for large welfare benefits and a characteristically conservative proposal for small welfare benefits. Predictably, liberals preferred the first proposal and conservatives preferred the second proposal. Cohen then presented a second group of partisans with the same proposals but told them which party supported and opposed the policies. It turns out that labels trump substance: liberals favored the conservative policy when told it had Democratic support and conservatives favored the liberal policy when told it had Republican support. Cohen writes: "For both liberal and conservative participants, the effect of reference group information overrode that of policy content. If their party endorsed it, liberals supported even a harsh welfare policy and conservatives supported even a lavish one."[21] Notably, subjects appeared unaware of the influence of partisanship on their judgments, insisting that they evaluated the policies on the basis of their "philosophy of government" and the policies' merits.[22]

We see something similar in partisans' real-world policy evaluations. For instance, Republican support for free trade agreements fell by 20% between 2015 and 2017—a period which saw the election of a Republican president hostile to free trade.[23] And as you might expect, Democrats' support for free trade *rose* during that same period.[24]

In 2009, at the start of the administration of Barack Obama, a Democrat, 64% of Democrats expressed confidence in Federal Reserve Chairman Ben Bernanke, compared to only 36% of Republicans.[25] However, just one year earlier the confidence ratings of the very same person were almost exactly reversed—61% of Republicans were confident in Bernanke compared to 40% of Democrats.[26] So what changed in the span of a single year? You guessed it: in the previous year, Bernanke was serving under a Republican president. More generally, most Americans exhibit an "absence of stable views independent of party," a pattern that "seems most consistent with widespread following, or voters adopting views consistent with their preferred political party or leader."[27] Here again, we see that the motivation of our political beliefs tends not to be the discovery of truth but rather alignment with our political team.

That our policy preferences follow our partisan identity also explains the curious way in which our political beliefs cluster.[28] Consider that people who believe that a fetus has a right to life usually oppose gun control and support school vouchers. It's not clear that there is any meaningful philosophical connection between those three political beliefs. As philosopher Hrishikesh Joshi puts it, these issues are "rationally orthogonal"—the reasons in favor of your position on one of these issues are unrelated to the reasons in favor of your position on the others.[29]

A similar point applies to purely empirical debates—for instance whether humans are causing climate change or the effect of permitting concealed handguns on homicide rates. We are increasingly polarized over matters of fact, not simply values.[30] Professor of Law and Psychology Dan Kahan writes,

> Whether humans are heating the earth and concealed-carry laws increase crime, moreover, turn on wholly distinct bodies of evidence. There is no logical reason for positions on these two empirical issues—not to mention myriad others, including the safety of underground nuclear-waste disposal, the deterrent impact of the death penalty, the efficacy of invasive forms of surveillance to combat terrorism to cluster *at all*, much less form packages of beliefs that so strongly unite citizens of one set of outlooks and divide those of opposing ones. However, there is a *psychological* explanation. . . . That explanation is *politically motivated reasoning*.[31]

The evidence relevant to determining whether humans are causing global warming is not the same as the evidence that is relevant to determining whether gun control decreases crime. So why do people who doubt that humans cause global warming almost always doubt that gun control decreases crime as well? That is, what do skepticism about anthropogenic global warming and gun control have in common?

The answer is that skepticism about anthropogenic global warming and gun control are both part of what one particular political team stands for. Kahan continues,

> Where positions on some policy-relevant fact have assumed widespread recognition as a badge of membership within identity-defining affinity groups, individuals can be expected to selectively credit all manner of information in patterns consistent with their respective groups' positions. The beliefs generated by this form of reasoning excite behavior that expresses individuals' group identities. Such behavior protects their connection to others with whom they share communal ties.[32]

Republicans are motivated to reason in ways protective and expressive of their identities as Republicans and Democrats are motivated to reason in ways protective and expressive of their identities as Democrats. Their political viewpoints shape their interpretation of the facts—not the other way around.

THE CASE FOR HUMILITY

So what, exactly, is wrong with politically motivated reasoning? Why shouldn't you trust your political beliefs when you know you are in its grip? The reason, in short, is that even though you almost certainly have some false political beliefs, you won't correct these false beliefs in light of counterevidence. Rather, you'll figure out how to explain away the counterevidence to protect your identity as a good member of Team Democrat or Team Republican.

Let's work through this argument more carefully. Why should you think that you have some false political beliefs?

Given that there is little to no connection between the evidence for anthropogenic global warming, private gun ownership's deterrence impact on crime, the effect of tax cuts on economic growth, and so on, it would be quite the coincidence if all of the evidence converged to support the exact policy bundle advocated by Republicans and opposed by Democrats (or the exact policy bundle advocated by Democrats and opposed by Republicans). So the odds are high that you are wrong about at least some issues regardless of which side you are on.

Of course, having false beliefs isn't an insurmountable problem. You can correct them in light of the evidence. But the studies I've reviewed show that political partisans are generally unmoved by evidence. When confronted with information that threatens our side, we're masters at ignoring, downgrading, and discrediting it to maintain our partisan allegiance. Thus, even if the evidence points to our side being wrong, we'll continue to believe that we're right.[33]

Here's an analogy: suppose you have a compass that always points north, regardless of the direction you're headed.[34] You shouldn't trust that compass when it tells you that you're headed north. Why not? Because even though the compass might be correct, it's merely a lucky coincidence if it is. If you're actually headed south, you'd never know it from the compass.

Similarly, if your partisan brain always "points Republican," you should be hesitant to trust it. That is, you'll continue to believe that capital punishment is an effective deterrent regardless of whether it actually is effective because you're motivated to dismiss any information to the contrary. Your position might be right, but it's merely a lucky coincidence if it is. You won't correct it in light of evidence that the Democrats got it right. If the Democrats actually *are* right, you'd never believe it.

Here's the upshot: you should be humble about your political beliefs and appreciate the likelihood that many of them are wrong. Note that you can be humble about your answers to questions while still believing that there are correct answers to be found. I'm humble about my ability to answer the question "What's the number of grains of sand on Earth?" That doesn't mean I think all answers are equally good or that we have no way of figuring out what the correct answer is. It's just that I shouldn't be particularly confident that I know what the correct answer happens to be. Similarly, I'm not denying that some policies are better than others. I don't believe politics is just a matter of opinion in the way that the tastiest ice cream flavor is just a matter of opinion. Rather, I'm saying most of us are overconfident in our beliefs about complicated and controversial political issues.

Critically, if we have serious doubts about our political beliefs, we should have serious doubts that working to enact policies informed by these beliefs will make the world a better place. By analogy, if a doctor comes to the realization that she cannot trust her own judgment that a given drug will help rather than hurt her patient, she shouldn't prescribe it. She should, perhaps, prescribe a different drug—a drug in which her confidence is justified.

Along the same lines, if you come to the realization that you cannot trust your own judgment that a given policy will help rather than hurt people, you ought not to advocate for it. You should instead dedicate yourself to other moral causes in which your confidence is justified. As philosopher Michael Huemer explains,

> In many cases, the [political] effort is expended in bringing about a policy that turns out to be harmful or unjust.

It would be better to spend one's time and energy on aims that one *knows* to be good. . . . Donations to Moveon.org may or may not affect public policy, and if they do, the effect may be either good or bad—that is a matter for debate. But donations to Against Malaria *definitely* save lives. No one disputes that.[35]

While it might be too strong to claim that *no one* disputes the effectiveness of donations to the Against Malaria Foundation, it is safe to say that we should have far *more* confidence in the effectiveness of this charity and those like it than we have in the effectiveness of our favored political causes.[36]

MAYBE EVERYONE *ELSE* IS A PARTISAN HACK

At this point, you might be thinking that you're an exception to the rule. *Others* are vulnerable to politically motivated reasoning, but not you. Maybe you're more intelligent or better educated than most and so you're more resistant to bias.

Generally speaking, you should be wary of arguments made on behalf of self-exemption. To start, consider the "bias blind spot."[37] We tend to recognize the role of bias in the judgments of others, but not ourselves.[38] Moreover, learning about the pervasiveness of bias does not cause us to appreciate its effects on our own judgment.[39] Considering oneself an exception to the norm of bias is precisely what bias leads one to do.

Moreover, people of higher intelligence are *more* susceptible to the bias blind spot.[40] Intelligence also appears to amplify, rather than suppress, political bias. We use our cognitive skills to better defend our team rather than to consider issues more impartially. Consider a study that asked participants to render a judgment about a particular policy issue, such as whether increased public school funding would improve academic outcomes.[41] With the initial judgment in place, participants were asked to list all of the reasons they could muster on both sides of the issue. Participants produced far more arguments in support of their own position than against it.

Interestingly, while IQ was the best predictor of a participant's ability to produce arguments, it only predicted the ability to produce arguments in support of the participant's position. In short, the higher your IQ, the better you are at giving reasons on behalf of a position—so long as it's *your* position. As the researchers put it, "People invest their IQ in buttressing their own case rather than in exploring the entire issue more fully and evenhandedly."[42] Intelligence does not make you more fair-minded or less protective of your social identity. Rather people who are better at reasoning are "better" at politically motivated reasoning. (If you've taken a philosophy class, you know that skilled arguers can make a compelling case for nearly *any* conclusion, no matter how absurd.)

Perhaps the most famous study in this area concerns the effect of partisanship on mathematical performance.[43] Subjects were first presented with a description of an experiment on patients with skin conditions. They were told some patients used a skin cream while others did not. Subjects were then given information about the number of people in each group whose skin condition got better and those whose condition got worse. More people who used the cream saw their condition improve than those who did not use the cream. So, most subjects answered that those who used the cream were more likely to see improvement than those who did not. However, over twice as many people used the skin cream than did not. Even though more total users saw improvement than non-users, a higher *percentage* of non-users got better. Thus, the quick glance at the numbers was misleading. To get the correct answer, subjects needed to slow down and think the problem through. Unsurprisingly, those subjects who were better at math were more likely to arrive at the correct answer.

Here's the twist. The experimenters ran another variation of the experiment, substituting politically charged information for the politically neutral information about skin cream. Subjects surveyed statistics about crime in cities that banned handguns versus those that did not. In some cases, the statistics revealed that the ban reduced crime; in other cases, the statistics showed that the ban failed. Liberals did an excellent job of answering correctly when the correct answer revealed that gun control worked. When the correct answer was that gun control failed, they tended to get the answer wrong. The same result was found for conservatives, just reversed.

The truly astounding finding, however, is that those with high mathematical skill were 45 percentage points more likely to get the answer right when it affirmed, rather than challenged, their partisan commitment—compared to only a 25 percentage point difference for those with low mathematical skill.[44] More generally, people who score highest in cognitive reflection—roughly, deliberate and effortful reasoning—are the most likely to display politically motivated cognition.[45]

Education doesn't help much either. For instance, training subjects on logical reasoning didn't enable them to overcome their partisan bias in evaluating arguments.[46] Higher levels of science comprehension *increase* politically motivated reasoning about climate change.[47] Indeed, education seems to reinforce partisan commitments.[48]

You might be tempted by the following line of thought: "Look, I get it. Everyone is at least a little biased. But, come on, let's get real—[out-party members] are much worse about it than [in-party members]." Deep down, you just know that the other side is worse.

The trouble is, the evidence doesn't support this claim. Liberals and conservatives exhibit the same tendency toward identity-protective reasoning.[49] Both sides are resistant to identity-threatening scientific research.[50] Indeed, research indicates that people's assessment of the evidence for an asymmetry in a susceptibility to politically motivated reasoning is *itself* susceptible to politically motivated reasoning.[51] So I'm sorry to report that you're probably as biased as the rest of us.

IS IT HOPELESS?

Is it the case that there is *nothing* we can do to effectively fight against the gravitational pull of politically motivated reasoning? That conclusion might be too strong. But it's worth stressing that the most intuitive strategies for debiasing ourselves don't have solid empirical support.

For instance, you might naturally think that exposing yourself to the other side's arguments would soften your opposition and deepen your appreciation for their views. But hearing the other side sometimes—although not always—reinforces partisanship (it's uncertain exactly how often this occurs). For instance, subjects presented with negative information about their preferred candidate in a mock election viewed the candidate more positively.[52]

Although initially counterintuitive, this sort of result makes sense in light of the evidence presented earlier. Since we react to opposing viewpoints defensively—by trying to prove the other side wrong—exposing people to opposing viewpoints will serve to *increase* the number of arguments they have available to justify their own position and reject the other side.[53]

The track record of active discussion and deliberation about politics isn't promising either.[54] While there is some evidence that offering monetary incentives for accurate political beliefs can work, there is debate about how significant the effect is.[55] Some suggest that performing self-affirmation exercises make people more receptive to information, although here again, opinion is divided.[56]

However, there are some strategies that might be effective. Peter Coleman, a psychologist who runs the Difficult Conversations Lab at Columbia, suggests that political conversations can be structured in ways that make them more productive.[57] For instance, if you'd like discussants to make progress on the ethics of immigration, you can have them read a paper beforehand about a different but equally polarizing topic (say, euthanasia) that highlights its complexity (as opposed to a rigid for-and-against format). Then, ask them to work together to craft a statement about the contested issue that they can both endorse. Structuring conversations in this way appears to deepen people's appreciation for the nuance of an issue and increase their willingness to discuss it further.

You could also try to soften your partisanship by probing your own ignorance of public policy. In the previous chapter, I discussed the "illusion of explanatory depth"—most of us think we understand the world better than we actually do. At first people think they know how a particular policy works, but they downgrade their own understanding once they fail to give a detailed explanation of the policy's mechanics.[58] Crucially for present purposes, subjects' positions on the policies became more moderate after their failed explanations. This moderating effect was not found in subjects asked to give reasons why they support a policy rather than an explanation of how the policy works. So we might crack our partisan confidence by asking how our favored policies work, not why they are good ideas.

These findings suggest some strategies you can try if you want to chip away at your tendency toward politically motivated reasoning. You could force yourself to write a step-by-step account of the mechanics of Social Security funding and distribution. Next, you could check the accuracy of your account. Then you could repeat this process for all of the relevant policy proposals (foreign aid, campaign finance reform, environmental legislation, and so on). Finally, having destabilized your confidence in your beliefs about various policy matters, you could reevaluate their merits one by one.

You'll notice that this method of combatting politically motivated reasoning is expensive—it takes far more time and focus than passively watching CNN. Is the investment worth it? Probably not. For one, the jury is still out on these debiasing strategies. Although they show promise, the extent to which they will improve the accuracy of our political judgment remains uncertain.

Moreover, the benefit of implementing these strategies will often fail to justify the cost. Consider that it makes sense to take a methodical, labor-intensive, and time-consuming approach to studying for the SAT. The expected benefit of studying is high. By contrast, suppose your teacher tells you that she will distribute a pop quiz on course material tomorrow—but only if she wins the lottery tonight. Given how improbable it is that you'll end up taking the quiz, you have little reason to buckle down and study for it. Indeed, even only insofar as you care about your grade in that class, it would be irrational for you to study for the quiz. Your time is better spent on something else that will actually make a difference to your grade—polishing your upcoming essay, preparing impressive comments on the readings for the next class, and so on.

Similarly, if you know that there is only, say, a one in a billion chance that your vote, protest sign, or tweet will change political outcomes, then you have little reason to begin the methodical, labor-intensive, and time-consuming job of softening up your partisan bias. Indeed, as I'll argue next, even only insofar as you care about promoting justice and the common good, your time is better spent on nonpolitical endeavors that will more effectively advance those ends, such as taking direct action to shelter the homeless, feed the hungry, or enrich the poor.

Three

> By combining the heart and the head—by applying data and reason to altruistic acts—we can turn our good intentions into astonishingly good outcomes.
>
> —William MacAskill, *Doing Good Better*

Figuring out what's best in politics is hard. But if the impact of your political participation is great enough, the work may be worth it. Figuring out how to cure cancer is hard, but the payoff is so high that the investment of time and effort is justified.

The trouble is, your political participation probably won't make a difference. In typical cases, a single person's vote, protest, or letter to the editor won't change anything. Even if you happen to vote in a key swing state where there is a nontrivial chance that you could affect the electoral outcome, the expected social benefit of your vote remains low given how uncertain it is that your vote is actually aimed at the best result. Moreover, engaging in politics means passing up opportunities to engage in more effective forms of altruism, such as contributing to well-researched and high-impact charities that literally save lives.[1] In short, you can expect to do more good for the world by taking direct, nonpolitical action to help people rather than by participating in politics.

THE EFFECTIVENESS OF POLITICAL ACTION

Let's start with a case of political action whose impact is easy to quantify: voting. For your vote to bring about a change in the electoral outcome, it must make or break a tie. That is, the vote must be "decisive." Depending on the state that you vote in, the probability of casting a decisive vote in the U.S. presidential election has been estimated to be as high as 1 in 10 million or as low as in 1 in a billion.[2]

Why are the odds so low? For your vote to make a difference to the outcome of a presidential election, two things have to happen. First, your state has to be necessary for the candidate to win the Electoral College. Second, your vote has to make or break a tie in your state. The odds of these two events occurring are surpassingly low.

California is a clear example. The state has 55 electoral votes, which is the most in the country. So flipping California with your vote very well could flip the national election. But what are the odds of that? In the 2016 presidential election, there were about 14 million votes cast in the state. For your vote to break a tie, then, roughly 14 million votes would need to be split exactly 50/50 between the two major party candidates. Needless to say, it's not going to happen. (Of course, the odds are better in different states—I'll return to this point at the end of the chapter.)

Indeed, even if your vote does defy the odds and makes or breaks a tie, the result would be a recount. And if history is any guide, a razor-thin margin of victory will send the election to the courts. As Stephen Dubner and Steven Levitt note,

> The closer an election is, the more likely that its outcome will be taken out of the voters' hands—most vividly exemplified, of course, by the 2000 presidential race. It is true

that the outcome of that election came down to a handful of voters; but their names were Kennedy, O'Connor, Rehnquist, Scalia and Thomas. And it was only the votes they cast while wearing their robes that mattered, not the ones they may have cast in their home precincts.[3]

Thus, the outcome of even an extremely close presidential election will probably not be decided by your vote, but rather by lawyers and judges.

Moving to smaller elections doesn't change things significantly either. For instance, congressional races tend not to be competitive.[4] Sure, sometimes a race is decided by a single vote, but those cases are *extraordinarily* rare.[5] The moral of the story is that your vote will almost certainly never be decisive. Indeed, even those who defend a duty to vote often concede this point and so work to justify the duty on grounds other than the consequences of voting.[6]

Of course, voting is not the only form of political engagement. But the worry about ineffectiveness is going to apply to most of these other cases, too. Take participation in protests. What matters here is the *marginal* effect of your presence at the protest. That is, what would change if your individual appearance at the protest never happened? By way of example, the "March for Science," which advocated for an evidence-based approach to public policy, attracted over one million participants worldwide.[7] Would the impact of that march been any different if the total number of marchers had been, let's say, 1,072,438 instead of 1,072,439? No. So even if the March for Science has had an impact on public policy, the issue is *your* impact on the March for Science.[8] Since the march would be equally successful with or without you, your impact is effectively zero.

YOUR PARTICIPATION DOESN'T PROMOTE YOUR INTERESTS

The ineffectiveness of most political action undermines arguments that participation is a good way to serve your own interests or the interests of the public.

Let's start with one's own interests. Although participating to improve your own condition might not be a moral reason to participate, it could be a legitimate reason to participate nonetheless. After all, you have a legitimate reason to eat kale out of a concern for your own well-being even if it isn't a moral reason. Indeed, sometimes people are even admonished for voting against their interests. So long as advocating for your interests isn't out of line with the respect you owe to the interests of others, it seems to be at least morally permissible.[9]

But political participation isn't a smart way of promoting your own interests precisely because of its ineffectiveness.[10] While the outcomes of elections no doubt impact your interests, your participation tends to have little impact on those outcomes. You'd be better off ignoring the election and working overtime with the hours you would have spent researching and casting a vote, investing the extra income wisely, and letting compound interest work its magic.[11]

Maybe you're thinking that political participation serves your interests simply because you *enjoy* political participation. Fair enough. But this is analogous to my claim that cheering for the Philadelphia Eagles serves my interests simply because I enjoy cheering for them. The claim is true, but it's hardly applicable to the general population. It's a form of recreation that happens to suit me, but it's not for everyone.[12]

It might not make sense to participate if you only care about your own interests. But what if you care about *everyone's* interests?

A number of philosophers have argued that you should participate in politics because you have a (small) chance of significantly impacting a significant number of people. By analogy, Derek Parfit argues that a nuclear engineer ought to worry about a one-in-a-million chance of killing one million people.[13] Along the same lines, it could be rational for a voter to worry about a one-in-300 million chance of dramatically changing the shape of government for 300 million people. As Brian Barry puts it, if a voter "really gives full weight to the consequences for *everyone* that he expects will be affected, this will normally provide an adequate reason for voting."[14]

If the odds of bringing about a massively beneficial outcome are low enough, it is still not worth trying. Even those who argue that the expected social benefit of voting can be sufficiently high to justify voting in key swing states acknowledge that the probability of casting a decisive vote in other states is too low to make voting worthwhile even if the election of your favored candidate would be worth hundreds of billions of dollars.[15] By analogy, consider that you could do a monumental amount of good with the money you could win playing the Powerball lottery. Nevertheless, you shouldn't buy a lottery ticket because the probability of hitting the jackpot is too low.[16] And so it tends to go with your vote.

OTHER KINDS OF CONSEQUENCES

The insignificance of a single vote also undercuts other rationales for voting. Perhaps you ought to vote to contribute to a mandate.[17] You won't help the best candidate get elected, but you'll help her govern more effectively by increasing her margin of victory.

One worry about this argument is that there is reason to doubt that mandates exist.[18] In any case, the contribution an individual vote makes to the margin of victory is insignificant and thus unlikely to be more socially beneficial than the alternative uses of one's time.

Another persistent objection to the claim that your political participation is insignificant appeals to the potential for political behavior to influence others. Perhaps your participation—taken by itself—makes no difference, but we can't ignore the possibility that your presence at the protest will prompt others to join in. Your participation may have a ripple effect. This argument gains steam when we broaden our focus to political engagement more generally—taking an active interest in talking politics with others and encouraging their participation could make a difference over time. I've even had students say they'll forgive me for not voting so long as I have the decency to keep my abstention a secret, lest I become a bad influence on others. (I've told students if they are worried about my influence, I could always lie and tell people I'm politically active; a few have endorsed this option.)

This is my favorite objection because it's so flattering. Sadly, though, I'm just not that influential; you probably aren't either. (However, if this book becomes a runaway bestseller bringing me fame, fortune, and influence over American political culture, then I'll consider publicly repudiating my arguments for the greater good.) I know that I'm not very influential because I couldn't tell you how many conversations I've had with students that:

Student: Professor, you shouldn't tell people that they don't need to vote.

Me: Why not?

Student: You could end up encouraging political apathy and that's bad for the country.

Me: So have I persuaded you to not vote?

Student: Well, no.

Students can't even bring themselves to lie to me about my influence to butter me up! (Besides, if I really had that much influence over my students, I wouldn't receive so many late papers.) If anything, my personal experience leads me to believe that people react to my arguments by doubling down on their insistence on voting, if only to spite me.

Notice also that a good deal of political participation occurs in private. Sending in an absentee ballot or donating to a campaign is unlikely to induce others to do the same for the simple reason that they don't see you doing these things. Thus, if you're really concerned about your influence, then you'd need to make a public display of your political engagement. (You can also make public displays of your politics without formally participating in politics by, e.g., putting bumper stickers on your car—more on this point in Chapter 6.)

Lastly, consider the question of what kind of participation our influence will promote. Is the aim to simply encourage political participation as such or to encourage informed and unbiased participation? I assume the latter, but notice that the work needed to participate well is typically done outside of public view—reading, listening, deliberating, and so on. Merely standing in line at the polls won't influence others to do their homework when no one is watching.

LOCAL POLITICS

What about local politics? After all, you have a greater likelihood of flipping a mayoral election than a presidential election.

It's important to notice up front that your higher chance of making an impact comes with a cost—namely a lower payoff if you do make an impact. Causing your preferred candidate to get elected president is monumental; causing your preferred candidate to get elected dogcatcher is a shrug emoji. (And yes, there actually is a town where dogcatcher is an elected office.)[19]

Still, I wouldn't want to give the impression that local engagement can never help. Something as simple as advocating for getting a pothole fixed could make the world a marginally better place. But you can also make the world a better place via nonpolitical engagement. Indeed, you will typically be more effective if you spend the time you would have spent on local politics taking direct, nonpolitical action to solve local problems. If you see a pothole, you could simply circumvent the politics and fix it yourself like a neighborly vigilante.

EFFECTIVE ALTRUISM AND THE OPPORTUNITY COST OF POLITICAL PARTICIPATION

I've briefly alluded to the opportunity cost of political participation, but let's address this issue head on. You've probably heard that there's no such thing as a free lunch. This doesn't mean that you can't get a lunch without parting ways with your money. You can. The point is rather that you always have to give up something to get something—for instance, that lunch will take up time and stomach space.

Similarly, the portion of your life allocated to politics is a portion not allocated to other ways of helping others.[20] So a key reason to ignore politics is the opportunity cost of attending to politics—time spent watching debates, handing out pamphlets, and writing political Facebook posts is time not spent on endeavors that do more good.

To make the idea more vivid, consider a simple case. Suppose you're a single-issue voter: you only care about food insecurity. You're voting for the candidate that will do the most to feed America's hungry. While you're driving to the polls on a deserted country road, you notice someone with a cardboard sign that reads, "Please help." You pull over and ask her what help she needs. She says that the local soup kitchen closes in 20 minutes and she needs a ride or else she'll go hungry yet again. Unfortunately for you, the polls *also* close in 20 minutes. So you can either drive her to the soup kitchen or vote for your favored candidate.

The right thing for you to do is to not vote but rather drive her to the soup kitchen. Voting will not result in anyone getting fed who otherwise wouldn't. But driving her will result in someone getting fed who otherwise wouldn't. Insofar as you value feeding the hungry, you should drive her to the soup kitchen instead of driving yourself to the polls.[21] The opportunity cost of voting well won't always be this obvious, of course. But the point illustrated in the case stands: the expected social benefit of private humanitarianism will typically exceed the expected social benefit of humanitarian voting.

More specifically, I recommend forgoing political engagement for what has come to be called *effective altruism*. Philosophers such as Peter Singer and William MacAskill argue that we should use the best available evidence to direct our philanthropic efforts to the causes that are the most effective at helping people.[22] Examples of effective altruism include efforts to prevent malaria, support deworming programs, and distribute cash directly to the global poor.[23] These programs do more good per dollar donated than any others.

By way of example, a rough estimate of the lowest cost required to save a "quality adjusted life year" is $68.90 (if one donates to the Against Malaria Foundation).[24] The average American hourly wage in 2018 was about $22.50.[25] So, at the risk of oversimplifying, working three hours of overtime enables you to earn enough donatable income to save a year of human life. Thus, we have an astonishing opportunity to help others. But notice how the presence of these high-impact charitable alternatives weakens the case for political participation: the opportunity cost of three hours dedicated to politics is approximately one year of human life.[26]

POLITICAL ACTION AND NONPOLITICAL ACTION: WHY NOT DO BOTH?

One natural objection to my defense of nonpolitical moral engagement will grant that nonpolitical engagement is morally required but argue that it's required in addition to—not instead of—political engagement. You should do both. Political scientist Julia Maskivker argues that we do not morally excuse ourselves from voting by contributing to other sorts of social goods just as we do not morally excuse ourselves from giving a particular stranded woman change for a bus ride by performing a different charitable act.[27] Maskivker argues that a duty of "easy aid" obliges us to help the woman—you can assist the woman without unduly burdening yourself, and so it seems like you ought to assist her.[28]

Similarly, in Maskivker's view, "the duty to vote with care" is "not unreasonably burdensome because it is episodic" and does not require an "overwhelming commitment to politics."[29] Moreover, elections

> constitute a structure that situates us in a perfect position to render help easily. Assuming minimal efficiency and

transparency, the machinery of elections emerges in front of you for you to vote and vanishes shortly after the choice period is over.[30]

Thus, you're obligated to vote with care just as you are obligated to assist the woman—you are in a position to help at a low (and non-repeating) cost to yourself. That you are obligated to assist the woman doesn't imply that you are not obligated to also give to charity; similarly, that you are obligated to vote with care doesn't imply that you are not obligated to also give to charity.

The problem with analogizing voting well to "easy aid" is that it is neither easy nor is it typically a form of effective aid. Let's revisit the effectiveness point. One consideration that grounds an obligation to help the woman is that

> the good of sparing the woman a homeless night trumps the cost (i.e. the two coins). By the same token, society needs our help now (child poverty, anyone?) and elections exist so that we can provide such help relatively easily, and our cost being no more than the acquisition of available information (If we would rather avoid the lines at the polling booths, we can always send the ballot by post). To ignore this confluence of factors, I would say, is morally wrong.[31]

Notice, though, that the expected good of your *vote* does not usually trump the cost for the reasons already given. And this is a crucial disanalogy. (In response to this sort of worry, Maskivker suggests that we can also understand a duty of aid as a duty to contribute to highly beneficial collective activities even when the expected benefit of an individual contribution is low—I'll say more about this style of argument in the next chapter.)[32]

You might be thinking to yourself: "I only have a handful of chances to vote and, really, what do I have to do in that specific hour that is more helpful?" But the answer is simple: lots of things! Here's an idea—start an Election Day tradition of making and soliciting donations to the Against Malaria Foundation.

When I make this argument in conversations, people often reply that they simply won't engage in nonpolitical altruism instead of political engagement. But I confess that this response puzzles me. It doesn't discredit the claim that effective donating tends to do more good than a vote; rather, it suggests that my interlocutor isn't really *that* interested in doing good on Election Day. Consider:

Doctor: You're in bad health. You really should eat more vegetables.

Patient: Well, I'm not going to do that. I'll tell you what, though: I will start taking this UltraHealth diet pill I got online.

Doctor: That's just a fancy sugar pill—it won't make you any healthier. You need to eat vegetables.

Patient: I hear you Doc, but I'm still going with the pill.

That the patient will consume the pill but not the broccoli doesn't discredit the doctor's claim that eating the broccoli is healthier than taking the pill; it just shows that the patient isn't *that* interested in getting healthy.

Here's a second worry about the "episodic voting is easy" point. Merely voting may only take an hour or so at periodically available, formally arranged times, but voting with *care* takes a much larger commitment of time and energy. By analogy, it's false that "answering SAT questions with care" is an easy thing to do simply because the SAT only requires a few hours at periodically available, formally arranged times. The *real* investment takes place long before the test. Similarly, the real investment in voting takes place long before the polls open. Doing it with care is costly, which in turn soaks up more resources from other moral endeavors. Maskivker concedes that voting with care requires that we obtain "minimal information," but I've argued that we tend to underestimate the work needed to make our vote a good one.[33]

ON IGNORING THE ROOT CAUSES OF INJUSTICE

One popular criticism of effective altruism alleges that it focuses on the individual at the expense of the system. For instance, 15 economists (including three Nobel Prize winners) object that devoting ourselves to "micro-interventions at a local level" does "little to change the systems that produce the problems in the first place. What we need instead is to tackle the real root causes of poverty, inequality and climate change."[34] Philosopher Paul Gomberg says that promoting individual altruism "promotes political quietism" and shifts "our focus from political, social, and economic issues to abstract philosophical arguments."[35] Philosopher Amia Srinivasan makes a similar argument:

> If everything comes down to the marginal individual, then our ethical ambitions can be safely circumscribed; the philosopher is freed from the burden of trying to understand the mess we're in, or of proposing an alternative vision of how things could be.[36]

I've never found this style of objection persuasive for a simple reason: I *am* the marginal individual. This fact seems relevant when I'm trying to figure out what I, the marginal individual, should do. As philosopher Jeff McMahan puts the point,

I am neither a community nor a state. I can determine only what I will do, not what my community or state will do. I can, of course, decide to concentrate my individual efforts on changing my state's institutions, or indeed on trying to change global economic institutions, though the probability of my making a difference to the lives of badly impoverished people may be substantially lower if I adopt this course than if I undertake more direct action, unmediated by the state.[37]

Acknowledging the limits of our individual impact and acting accordingly does not imply the moral insignificance of systemic problems; rather, it's a sober recognition of the reality of our situation. If you can ameliorate the effects of something harmful but not the root cause, then by all means ameliorate the effects.[38]

By analogy, boarding your windows, evacuating town, and setting up shelter for displaced residents before a hurricane hits does not imply that you endorse "quietism" about the hurricane. Rather, you are simply responding rationally to that which is in your control (mitigating some of the harmful effects of the hurricane) and that which is not (whether or not the hurricane strikes). Criticizing poverty relief for not addressing the root cause of poverty is like criticizing hurricane relief for not addressing the root cause of hurricanes.

Philosopher G.A. Cohen argues that institutional and political injustices may indeed be the *fundamental* injustices but suggests that the preventable poverty that arises from these structural injustices is itself an injustice. Cohen asks why someone in a position to help alleviate poverty should

not address the accessible injustice that he can address, even if it is a secondary one, by using his surplus income in the requisite way? It would be grotesque for him to say to those who lose from the unjust power division: "I won't succour you, since what I deplore is, at root, not your poverty, but the system that makes you poor."[39]

Indeed, consider how strange the argument made by critics of effective altruism looks when applied to other problems. Back to the doctor:

Patient: Hey Doc, I've got a terrible cold. Could you prescribe me a decongestant?

Doctor: No. A decongestant just treats your symptoms and alleviates your suffering. It would be a mistake to ignore the underlying cause.

Patient: OK—so you've got a cure for my cold?

Doctor: Well, no.

Patient: But if you spend a lot of time working on a cure, you'll come up with one?

Doctor: Almost certainly not.

Patient: So can you go ahead and prescribe that decongestant?

Doctor: No! Haven't you been listening?

I doubt this doctor would get many return patients. If our doctor is unable to cure our ailment, we expect her to at least treat the symptoms.

Let me also emphasize that critics of effective altruism are vulnerable to their own version of the neglect worry—namely, that a focus on systemic change will cause people to neglect those harms they *can* prevent through individual action. We ought to resist the comfort afforded by the thought that we have done our part by simply casting a vote aimed at enriching the poor and feeding the hungry, thereby freeing us of the burden of pursuing nonpolitical but more effective means of advancing those same ends.

WHAT IF YOUR PARTICIPATION *CAN* MAKE A DIFFERENCE? THE CASE OF SWING STATE VOTING

There might be occasions where you *are* in a position to address the root cause of a social problem. Political engagement isn't always futile. Maybe you're a senator or have a high likelihood of becoming one.[40]

A more interesting possibility is that you're a voter in a key swing state. Here the odds of your vote affecting the outcome of the presidential election are about 1 in 10 million, which are high enough to lead some philosophers and social scientists to suggest that casting a vote can be effective altruism.[41] Indeed, MacAskill—whom I agree with wholeheartedly on matters of charitable giving—argues that "voting for the better party is often an (expected) high-impact altruistic activity."[42]

To make this argument, MacAskill stipulates a "hypothetical $1,000 figure of the benefit per person of the better party being in power. If so, the total benefit to all Americans is $1,000 multiplied by the US population of 314 million, so $314 billion."[43] If you happen to live in a swing state like New Hampshire, it could be the case that

> voting is like donating thousands of dollars to (developed-world) charities. For all but the ultrarich, that's a much better use of your time than you could get, for example, by working the hour it takes you to vote and donating your earnings.[44]

So: should New Hampshirites vote even though Californians shouldn't?

I have my doubts. For one, MacAskill errs in putting the opportunity cost of voting at an hour or so of your time. This is a dramatic underestimate. Perhaps it takes an hour to register, drive to the polls, cast a vote, and drive home. But it takes considerably longer than an hour to undertake the relevant research and apply the relevant debiasing strategies.[45] Thus, the opportunity cost of an informed and unbiased vote is far higher than one hour's worth of labor income.

Second, in MacAskill's words, "the total benefit per American was a purely hypothetical number, so it should be taken with a grain of salt."[46] I'm not saying that the $314 billion figure misses the mark. I have no idea if it does or not. And that's precisely the problem.

MacAskill notes that uncertainty lowers the expected value of swing state voting:

> If you're uncertain about which party is really better, you might reasonably think it's an overestimate: your expected value of voting will be lower due to a greater chance of voting for the worse party; and if you're completely unsure which party is better the expected value of voting drops to zero.[47]

Along similar lines, Loren Lomasky and Geoffrey Brennan write that the value of a vote "must be discounted not only by the probability of being decisive but, additionally, by the probability that one has overestimated or even reversed the respective merits" of the candidates.[48] They call this *epistemic discounting*.[49]

To see how the problem of epistemic discounting weakens MacAskill's case for swing state voting, suppose I made the following claim: if you expect one design for a nuclear reactor to be $314 billion better than the other, then it's worth your time to advocate for that design. It still doesn't follow that it's worth your time to advocate for a particular design. Why not? Because you might have no clue which design is better. You should only advocate for a nuclear reactor design if your assessment of the comparative quality of nuclear reactor designs is justified. Otherwise, the rational thing to do is suspend judgment and allocate your time and resources to pursuits other than nuclear reactor design advocacy. Since most of us do not have justified assessments of the comparative quality of nuclear reactor designs, most of us should not advocate for a particular nuclear reactor design.

Similarly, MacAskill's argument shows that swing state voting is effective altruism only in cases where voters have (sufficiently high) justified confidence in their assessment of the comparative quality of the two major party presidential candidates. I've spent the previous two chapters arguing that most of us lack justified confidence in our political assessments. Here I agree with Lomasky and Brennan:

> Although the appropriate rate of epistemic discounting will vary from election to election and, of course, from voter to voter, in virtually all real-world election scenarios and for the vast majority of voters, it will be large enough to bring the [expected social benefit of voting] very close to zero. That is because political uncertainties are not all of one species but several, and they compound each other.[50]

Let's briefly review some of the sources of political uncertainty. To start, one candidate is probably better than the other in some ways, and vice versa.[51] Judging which candidate is better all things considered takes significant research and analysis that most of us have not done. If your intuition is that one candidate is better than the other on virtually all policy questions, recall my earlier argument about the politically convenient ways in which unrelated policy beliefs cluster. People who support school vouchers tend to also support private gun ownership and abortion restrictions; people who oppose school vouchers tend to also support gun control and abortion access. Yet the moral and empirical issues relevant to evaluating one of these policies are distinct from the moral and empirical issues relevant to evaluating the others. The thought that the one party gets it all right and the other party gets it all wrong on issues that have little, if anything, to do with each other is likely the product of reasoning aimed at political self-defense rather than truth.

Moreover, are the ways in which the Democrat is better than the Republican more important than the ways in which the Republican is better than the Democrat? Suppose one candidate is better on education but the other is better on immigration. Which of those two issues is weightier? And how much better on the various dimensions will the respective candidates be?

Other questions remain. Even if we know the policies that the different candidates advocate, how trustworthy are the candidates? After all, presidents routinely break their campaign promises.[52] Assuming the candidates *are* trustworthy, how effective will they be in carrying out their promises in the current political landscape?

If you're still attracted to the thought that the election of your preferred candidate really is worth $314 billion, ask yourself this question: have you ever actually sat down and done any *math* to calculate the benefits of each candidate when deciding who to vote for? Even if you have done the math, you probably should be skeptical of your results—remember that our math skills falter when we're crunching politically charged numbers.[53]

Indeed, consider what it would take to even go about making such a calculation. You'd need a good sense of the long-term, global effects resulting from each candidates' changes to policies concerning criminal justice, abortion, immigration, trade, taxation, entitlement spending, environmental protection, education, foreign policy, and many more. As noted earlier, most of us have neither the relevant policy information nor the competence to assess it.

You might think I'm exaggerating how difficult it is to form an impression of the better candidate (surely it's easier than a comparative analysis of nuclear reactor designs!). But you should resist that thought. After all, when we're talking about running a cost-benefit analysis of competing presidential candidates, we're talking about estimating how different packages of large-scale changes to a complex system with countless moving parts are going to play out on a global level over a number of years. As discussed in the first chapter, even experts have poor predictive track records. To think that we can make a remotely confident estimate of the specific dollar amount of a prospective president's long-term impact on millions (if not billions) of people is, in a word, optimistic.

Here again, let me reemphasize that the social science indicates that most of us are indeed overconfident in our political beliefs. We tend to have a poor understanding of how policies work even though we think we understand.[54] We also tend to have a poor understanding of the effectiveness of policies.[55] I know it *seems* like your side is clearly right, but that's probably because you selectively affirm information that supports your side and selectively reject information that threatens it. Given what we know about our vulnerability to politically motivated reasoning, we should guard against the understandable-but-unjustified hunch that aiming our vote at the best candidate is an easy task. ("I don't need to put in a lot of time researching my vote—the [in-party] candidate is obviously the right choice. All of the evidence speaks in favor of her and against her opponent.") Politically motivated reasoning can delude us into thinking that all of the evidence is on our side even when it isn't. Our assessments of empirical evidence relevant to determining a policy's effectiveness—an indispensable consideration when running a cost-benefit analysis—are biased by our partisan commitments.[56] And we've seen that attempts to bypass one's own calculations of the cost and benefits of the candidates by deferring to an expert are similarly plagued by partisan bias.[57]

Consider also that MacAskill's argument implies that a vote for the wrong candidate in a swing state carries a meaningful risk of producing great harm. If there is a sufficiently high risk that your action will cause significant harm, it is reasonable to err on the side of caution and not perform that action.

In support of this thought, consider an example from philosopher Michael Huemer:

Imagine that I see a woman at a bus stop opening a bottle of pills, obviously about to take one. Before I decide to snatch the pills away from her and throw them into the sewer drain, I had better be very certain that the pills are actually something harmful. If it turns out that I have taken away a medication that the woman needed to forestall a heart attack, I will be responsible for the results. On the other hand, if, due to uncertainty as to the nature of the drugs, I decide to leave the woman alone, and it later turns out that she was swallowing poison, I will *not* thereby be responsible for her death.[58]

If you have good reason to doubt your judgment about whether snatching the woman's pills will help her or hurt her, no one would blame you for *not* snatching them.

To give you a case that is closer to voting, I'll tell you my idea for a (bad) episode of the *Twilight Zone*. A strange button is discovered in Colorado. If it's a good button, pressing it will save the lives of 100 people who otherwise would have died. If it's a bad button, pressing it will kill 100 people who otherwise would have lived. You have compelling reason to doubt your judgment about whether the button is good or bad. Should you press the button?

To get a handle on this question, imagine that your roommate learns of the button but declines to press it. She thinks the risk of being responsible for the death of 100 innocent people is too great given her doubts about her judgment of the button, so she decides to volunteer at a local soup kitchen instead of making the drive to Colorado. I doubt that you would blame your roommate for volunteering at the soup kitchen instead of pressing the button (even if you personally might choose differently). Thus, it seems as though it is not *obligatory* to press the button.

This same reasoning should lead you to conclude that it is, at a minimum, not *obligatory* to cast a vote in a swing state. You have good reason to doubt your judgment that the election of your preferred candidate will bring about great benefits rather than grave harms.[59] Moreover, working to acquire a justified belief about the relative merits of the candidates takes away a substantial amount of time from other altruistic pursuits such as earning income to donate to effective charities. In light of these considerations, it is morally acceptable to decide not to vote in a swing state and dedicate your spared time to nonpolitical altruism instead.

To summarize, here's where I land on swing state voting. If you haven't made a concerted effort to inform and debias yourself, then you should reserve judgment about which candidate is better and forgo voting in favor of nonpolitical altruism. On the other hand, you might intend to use the sort of evidence-based strategies for sharpening your political judgment discussed in the previous chapter. If your unsentimental calculation suggests that the opportunity cost of performing these time- and labor-intensive activities is sufficiently low, then I won't object too loudly if you go to the polls (after you've done your political homework).

On that note, let me stress how limited even a successful reconstruction of MacAskill's argument turns out to be. It would not show that there is a general obligation to vote.[60] At most, voting would be effective altruism in very specific conditions that are rarely met.

Think of it this way: everyone is under a moral obligation to not murder. It doesn't matter whether you live in California or New Hampshire or whether you know economics—don't murder. But an obligation to vote, even in the most optimistic scenario, wouldn't be like this. Rather, you'd only have an obligation to vote if you live in a critical swing state, vote for a major party candidate, do the methodical work needed to warrant confidence in your judgment of the candidates, and pay a sufficiently low cost to do that work.

Thus, the duty to vote would be similar to the duty of a scientist at a laboratory to research a cure for a deadly disease. The duty to research a cure is not a *general* duty that all, or even most, of us have. Rather, some people are in a special position

to do good and therefore may be under a special moral obligation. But just as most of us are not medical researchers, most of us are not among the debiased New Hampshire political cognoscenti. So the fact remains: it's highly unlikely that voting is the best use of your time.

Four

There's more than one way to create change.
—Colin Kaepernick, explaining why he doesn't vote

Your political participation is unlikely to make the world a better place. But maybe you should participate for reasons that have little to do with improving policy outcomes. Perhaps it's wrong to stay home on Election Day because you shouldn't "free ride" on the votes of your fellow citizens. It's not fair that they take the time to elect a good candidate while you settle in for a nap.

Fairness arguments for a duty to participate are among the most popular; however, they face obstacles both in principle and in practice. In principle, there's no reason why citizens can't do their part for society through nonpolitical contributions. As noted earlier, 49ers quarterback Colin Kaepernick was criticized for not voting in the 2016 presidential election while at the same time being a high-profile activist, but his response to the critics was spot on: voting isn't the only way to change the world for the better.[1] For instance, charitable donations of the sort Kaepernick himself made contribute to the common good—indeed, they tend to contribute more than political participation. (In the case of Kaepernick's own donations of over a million dollars, they contributed far more than his vote would have.)[2] In practice, fairness arguments rely on an unrealistic picture of political behavior. Many citizens don't make any political contributions at all. Those that do contribute tend to make ill informed and highly biased contributions which do not obligate you to reciprocate with contributions of your own.

THE GENERALIZATION ARGUMENT

Let's start with the most common objection to political abstention: "Sure, nothing will go wrong if you *alone* ignore politics, but the result would be disastrous if *everyone* ignored politics. So, it is wrong for you to ignore politics." Following philosophers Loren Lomasky and Geoffrey Brennan, let's call this the *generalization argument*.[3]

The "what if everybody did that?" objection is an intuitive one. We often make this objection in our everyday lives. ("Yes, I know that one gum wrapper won't spoil the beauty of these woods, but imagine if everyone littered. Pick it up.") Moreover, some prominent moral theories employ something approximating the generalization argument to assess the morality of an action.[4]

According to the simplest version of the generalization argument, the mere fact that it would be bad if everyone did X (or failed to do X) implies that it would be wrong for you as an individual to do X (or fail to do X). We can dispense with this version of the argument rather quickly. When I'm deciding whether or not I should be politically active, I'm trying to figure out what I should do, here and now, with the world as it is. It's not the case that everyone else is abstaining, nor will my decision to abstain cause everyone else to abstain. Since there is no chance that my choice to abstain will *actually* bring about disastrous consequences, the question motivating the generalization argument looks irrelevant.

Consider that the simplest version of the generalization argument is subject to an endless series of counterexamples.[5] If no one solved crimes, the results would be terrible. Criminals would be undeterred from committing crimes, and they would never receive the punishment they deserve. However, that the results would be terrible if no one solved crimes does not imply that you are obligated to become a detective. As things stand, plenty of people are solving crimes and so you're free to pursue a different occupation. Similarly, if no one delivered mail, taught children how to read, or distributed heart medication, the results would be terrible. But you're not obligated to become a postal worker, kindergarten teacher, or pharmacist.

My reply to the generalization argument also illuminates why my objections to a duty of political participation should not be construed as an objection to the institution of democracy. Democracy can be a valuable institution even if you, as a particular individual, are under no obligation to contribute to it. By analogy, fire departments are valuable institutions, but it is not the case that everyone is obligated to become a volunteer firefighter.

FREE RIDING

A promising variation on the generalization argument defends political participation on the grounds that your participation is required to avoid free riding on the participation of others.[6] According to this interpretation, the mere fact that it would be bad if everyone failed to X isn't what obligates you to X. Rather, you're obligated to do your fair share in providing certain sorts of social goods. When others are doing their part, you should do yours, too.

By way of example, I find myself chaperoning one of my children to a birthday party at least once a month. That's a lot of bounce houses, high fructose corn syrup, and small talk with strangers that I wouldn't mind skipping. But when my children's birthdays roll around, I want their parties to be well attended. Intuitively, I'd be doing something wrong by insisting that other families attend my own children's parties while exempting myself from attending the parties of their children.

Similarly, when you stay on your couch on Election Day, you are exploiting the political work of those who *do* go to the polls. Politically active citizens are putting in the effort to ensure that public schools function properly, that the air is clean, and that the country is safe. It wouldn't be fair if you benefited from those contributions without making a contribution of your own.[7]

Crucially, considerations of fairness obligate you to contribute even when your individual contribution is insignificant. Philosopher David Estlund offers an analogy:

> Suppose that if enough of us arrayed ourselves at the edge of town at midnight on the first day of each month, we could deter a dangerous gang from moving in (that is when they would otherwise try). It is virtually certain that my presence will not make or break the effort. There will either be enough people or not, but it will not depend on a single person. Still, I think there is clear moral reason to join this effort. Of course, some people can be excused if they have more important things to do, but there is a significant moral claim on them that would need to be overridden. In a similar way, there are disasters kept at bay by enough

people thoughtfully going to the polls, and there are serious reasons to join that effort, even though they can certainly sometimes be overridden by other weighty matters.[8]

Even though your presence at the edge of town will not "make or break" the deterrence effort, it still seems like you ought to show up, barring extenuating circumstances. Similarly, you ought to show up at the polls even though your vote probably won't make a difference to the outcome of the election.

ABSTENTION AND FREE RIDING: A PRELIMINARY REMARK

Before moving to my main replies, it's worth noting that political abstention is importantly different from other forms of abstention. When you don't pitch in for a neighborhood picnic, you thereby make others worse off—they have to pick up your share of the burden. But, as Lomasky and Brennan argue, when you don't vote, you actually *benefit* voters by amplifying the power of their vote.[9]

Lomasky and Brennan compare the nonvoter to someone ("Dalrymple") who decides to stop farming to become a dentist.[10] They make two observations about Dalrymple's decision. First, when she stops farming, she doesn't thereby treat her fellow farmers unfairly. To the contrary, they benefit from having one fewer farmer to compete with. Second, at the societal level, we need not worry that Dalrymple's departure from farming will induce others to depart and thus unravel the entire profession of farming. As a result of her departure, the remaining farmers can expect marginally higher wages, an outcome that will draw new farmers into the profession and offset the loss of Dalrymple's production.

The same sort of analysis applies to political abstention. When you decide not to vote, you slightly increase your neighbor's odds of casting a pivotal vote. Think of it this way: if everyone stopped voting except for you, you'd be guaranteed to pick the winner of the election. (Thus, the correct response to the objection, "What if everyone stopped voting?" is "In that case, I'd study hard and vote.") Political abstention, then, is unlike free riding in a morally significant respect—it benefits contributors rather than harms them. Second, as voters drop out and the impact of an individual vote increases, we should expect the increase in the value of a vote to draw new voters in—thereby avoiding universal abstention.[11]

To be clear, I don't take this analogy between political and economic contributions to show decisively that it's fair for you to abstain from politics. One worry about this line of argument is that it lets citizens off the hook too easily.[12] Do you really "contribute" to the common good by doing nothing when doing nothing happens to have a beneficial side effect? You might have your doubts.[13] So worries about free riding remain even if your abstention benefits political participants in one particular respect.

THE MORAL SIGNIFICANCE OF NONPOLITICAL CONTRIBUTIONS

Let's grant that you must actively contribute to the common good to pitch in your fair share. The pivotal question is this: must your contribution be distinctively *political* in form? After all, you can serve the public interest through teaching, writing, art, science, philanthropy, and more. As philosopher David Schmidtz writes, "Any decent mechanic does more for society by fixing cars than paying taxes."[14] Geoffrey Brennan and Loren Lomasky worry that funneling additional resources into political participation rather than alternative activities would be inefficient.[15]

Jason Brennan has argued at length that it is perfectly permissible to honor your obligation to contribute to the common good without contributing to politics in particular. Some citizens do their part for society

> by providing good governance, others by providing good culture, and others by providing economic opportunity. Citizens who provide these other kinds of goods are not free-riding on the provision of good governance. Rather, they pay for that good with a different kind of good.[16]

Someone who gives their community a beautiful mural is no less of a contributor than someone who casts a vote. Thus, Brennan argues, even if making a political contribution is one way you can avoid free riding, it is not the *only* way.

The question before us, then, is this: if you make your fellow citizens better off with your nonpolitical contributions to society, have you done your civic duty to promote the general welfare? Do you still need to make a political contribution in particular?

One reason for doubting that you need to make a distinctively political contribution is that cases in which you are obligated to reciprocate "in kind" are the exception, not the rule. When your friend helps you pack up for a move across town, you can reciprocate by buying them dinner. If a neighbor helps tutor your son in math, you can give them a Starbucks gift certificate. When someone delivers pizza to your door, you aren't obligated to deliver pizza to their door in return. You can give them a cash tip.

Along these lines, consider the following case from philosopher Jianfeng Zhu.[17] John's neighbors gather every Saturday to clean the community's walkways. Although John uses these walkways, he doesn't help clean them. But notice the reason why he doesn't participate:

> John refuses to participate in the scheme because he loves making cakes and Saturday is the only time available for him to try new recipes. But soon after the scheme starts to run, John realizes that he has been free riding. He then comes up with the idea that he should make more cakes on Saturday afternoon and put them in the community center for his participating neighbors to enjoy. It turns out that his neighbors love his cakes very much.[18]

I agree with Zhu that John repays his debt to his neighbors by baking them cakes, assuming the costs he bears and the benefits he provides are roughly equal to those of his neighbors.[19] John has made a perfectly satisfactory contribution to his community even though he didn't contribute in the same way as his neighbors.

The challenge for the fairness argument for political participation is this: if we can often repay our fellow citizens without in-kind reciprocity, why don't our nonpolitical contributions repay our debts to politically active citizens? What makes politics morally special, such that the beneficiaries of political goods must reciprocate with distinctively political contributions of their own?

EFFICIENCY AND THE DIVISION OF LABOR

Before I explore some reasons why fairness might require us to provide political contributions in particular, let me put in an additional word for nonpolitical contributions. In his illuminating discussion of how to most effectively tackle the problem of global poverty, philosopher Jeff McMahan emphasizes that "there has to be a certain division of moral labor, with some people taking direct action to address the plight of the most impoverished people, while others devote their efforts to bringing about institutional changes through political action."[20] Given that many millions of people are taking political action, taking nonpolitical action is the best use of your time.

Consider an analogy. Suppose we're on a camping trip where everyone has plenty of water to drink. I'm debating what kind of contribution to offer. I can make a costly-but-needless trip to the well or I can do something else that satisfies an unmet need, like gather firewood. At a minimum, it's permissible to not fetch water and gather firewood instead. Gathering firewood is a perfectly fine contribution to the trip; I am not guilty of free riding on the work of the campers who collected water simply because my contribution takes a different form. Indeed, it seems to me clearly *preferable* to gather firewood. Given that sufficient water has been collected, getting more water doesn't do any good. So doing something else with my time, like gathering the firewood, makes a more valuable contribution.

The same point applies to political abstention. Political activity is no different from other occupations such as delivering the mail: just as it would be inefficient for everyone to deliver the mail, it is inefficient for everyone to be politically active. Adding one more sign to the protest won't effectively promote the common good, so it's better to spend your time on something that will effectively promote the common good such as volunteering or earning money to donate. The division of labor that works on the camping trip works in society more generally.[21]

THE CASE FOR POLITICAL CONTRIBUTIONS

Political scientist Julia Maskivker rejects the idea that the contributions people make in their roles as farmers, teachers, and doctors are analogous to the contributions they make in their political roles.[22] For one, these economic contributions are motivated by self-interest instead of moral duty. As Adam Smith says, "It is not from the benevolence of the butcher, the brewer, or the baker that we expect our dinner, but from their regard to their own interest."[23] To put the point bluntly, the baker feeds you not because she cares about your interests, but because she cares about her own interests—interests that your money happens to serve.

More generally, people tend not to get moral credit for their self-interested contributions to the welfare of others. Consider:

Omar: Hey Rachel, are you going to join us tonight to work on the community garden?
Rachel: No, I think I'll skip it.
Omar: Really, why is that?
Rachel: Well, do you remember that boat I sold you last week?
Omar: Yes, what about it?
Rachel: I figure that by selling you that boat I've done my fair share for the community.
Omar: You mean that boat I gave you $30,000 for?
Rachel: That's the one!

Rachel shouldn't be excused from gardening simply because she provided Omar with benefits. She sold him the boat because the sale made her better off.

But this argument implies only that we need to make altruistic contributions to the common good, not political contributions.[24] Perhaps we don't get moral credit for the benefits we produce for others as by-products of actions motivated by self-interest. If you clothe people as part of your job at Target, you haven't made the right sort of contribution.[25] But if you clothe people during your time volunteering for a charitable organization, you've done your civic duty without going to the polls.

Consider another reason why nonpolitical altruism might be inadequate. As Maskivker argues, "Donating to charity (or any of a number of other acts) may be virtuous, but it does not affect the lives of every person as profoundly as selecting capable, civic-minded leaders."[26] It's true that private philanthropy typically doesn't affect as many lives as large-scale democratic governance. Even so, you may still have a stronger obligation to contribute to charity instead of good democratic governance. The math matters. Suppose I have $100 that I can use to either directly buy winter clothes for a family in need or buy 50 tickets for a $200 million lottery, with an expected value of $5. Playing the lottery gives me a chance of winning millions of dollars that I can, in turn, distribute to millions of people. But the odds of winning are extremely low. There's nothing wrong with spending the $100 directly on the family. I would go even further and say that it's wrong to play the lottery given that the expected philanthropic benefit of playing the lottery is significantly lower than the expected philanthropic benefit of direct help. In the same vein, the expected social benefit of political activism is typically lower than that of direct action, suggesting that you should allocate your resources to the latter.

Maybe the number of people impacted by political participation matters in a different way. Philosopher Brookes Brown notes that the scope of one's contribution is morally relevant, arguing that a payment of one's moral debt must be oriented (directly or indirectly) at the benefactor or benefactors whose behavior generated a debt. I cannot return the care a friend gives me when I am sick by helping my brother move. . . . Similarly, if Melissa, Joan, and H.L.A. Hart help change my tire, I cannot provide a fully fitting return by benefiting Melissa alone. I owe them all.[27]

Even if Rachel *gave* Omar the boat as thanks for his work on the community garden, she would still owe debts to the other members of the group. By the same reasoning, if you spend your weekend helping your politically active neighbor repair his deck, your debts to the other politically active members of your community remain unpaid.

Brown argues that we need to benefit all of our benefactors to honor our obligations. She notes,

> In *theory*, it is possible to pay civic debts through the direct provision of goods—a dollop of caviar here, a bottle of aspirin there, a Hawaiian shirt, a Humvee. In *practice*, however, this mechanism cannot fulfill civic debts. Our conationals are too numerous, their interests too divergent, to satisfy in this piecemeal fashion.[28]

The more practical option is to contribute to "universally desirable goods" that advance everyone's welfare.[29]

However, as Brown herself notes, this argument does not obligate us to undertake distinctively *political* actions. After all, we can contribute to "universally desirable goods such as public health, a clean environment, and safety" without engaging in politics.[30] Perhaps you further the cause of public health by distributing information about proper diet and exercise. Maybe you clean up the environment by saving money to buy an electric car and carbon offsets. You can donate to national hunger relief organizations that function as a kind of social insurance that helps citizens when they fall on hard times.[31]

WHAT'S A FITTING RETURN FOR POLITICAL PARTICIPATION?

Lawrence Becker's account of reciprocity provides an intriguing foundation for a duty of political participation. He suggests that you're obligated to deliver a *fitting* return for a good that someone has given you:

> Reciprocal exchanges are typically meant to sustain a particular practice or institution rather than productive social life *per se*. In that case, returns that are irrelevant to the special purpose so defined are not fitting, no matter how valuable they may be generally. (When someone needs help with the rent, an invitation to join a discussion group on the mating behavior of free ranging vervet monkeys will not do.)[32]

If you're driving across the country with friends and it's your turn to pony up for gas, you owe it to your friends to pay for gas. You don't get off the hook by knitting them sweaters even if the sweaters are of equal monetary value to the gas. You need to do your share in contributing to the particular purpose that everyone is contributing to.

Becker motivates the point with the following case.[33] Suppose that your life was saved by a blood transfusion that you received at a local blood bank. How could you repay those who donated blood to the bank? Becker suggests that attempting to find particular individuals and thank them would likely be inappropriate and unwelcome. And donating to another cause, no matter how worthy, doesn't do the trick either. The solution seems obvious: you ought to make your own contribution to the blood bank. As Becker puts it,

> If the benefit is not aimed at a specific person at all, but aimed instead at sustaining a social structure to provide such benefits to many people, we may conclude (in the absence of evidence to the contrary) that a return aimed at the same purpose will be fitting.[34]

So the idea here is not the flat-footed one that you must always reciprocate "in kind" but rather that working to sustain the institution from which you benefited and to which other people contributed is an appropriate form of reciprocity.

It seems as though a duty to make political contributions follows naturally from this argument. Take Jason Brennan's case of Phyllis, a brilliant medical researcher who looks to pay her debt to voters by producing medical breakthroughs in the lab while they are at the voting booth.[35] Becker's account suggests that Phyllis cannot repay the debt she owes to politically active citizens by advancing medical science. Voters, protestors, campaign donors, and so on work to advance political aims in particular; thus, a fitting return for their contribution to politics is one's own contribution to politics.

Even if Becker has the correct account of reciprocity, it would not generate a duty of political participation. On his view, a fitting return aims at the same purpose as the contribution of one's benefactor. But people may take different means to the same end. Think back to the blood bank. You need not donate blood to make a fitting contribution to the bank. Indeed, suppose the blood bank has plenty of blood, so donating more won't do much good. But one of their refrigerators has broken down and you offer to repair it. This seems like a perfectly fitting way of reciprocating for the blood donations of others. You contribute to the same purpose—ensuring that people have access to the blood they need—even though your contribution takes a different form.

Along the same lines, nonpolitical contributions can be a perfectly fitting return for political contributions. A donation to a food bank aims at the same purpose as a vote for policy that effectively combats food insecurity—namely, ensuring that the hungry have access to food. So you can do right by citizens who participate in politics if you work toward shared purposes in your private life.

I'll emphasize again that you can typically pursue the very same moral ends that participants pursue via politics more effectively via nonpolitical means. To appreciate the moral significance of this point, think back to Estlund's example of the collective effort to deter the gang that threatens your town. Your participation in that effort won't make a difference to its success; however, Estlund argues that you have a strong reason to participate nonetheless.

Let's flesh out the details of the case a bit further. Suppose you know that as the gang approaches, a single member of the gang will split off and attempt to rob your neighbor's house. What's more, the time, effort, and risk involved in (successfully) defending your neighbor equals the time, effort, and risk involved in joining the collective effort. Since you know your contribution won't make a difference to the success of the collective effort, you decide to fend off your neighbor's robber instead. My hunch is that the townspeople are more likely to say, "Good on you—that was smart!" than, "Shame on you for shirking!"

Note that your direct assistance to your neighbor better serves the end that your fellow townspeople are serving when they confront the gang. Their goal is to keep people in the town safe from crime. Your inconsequential contribution to their collective effort does nothing to advance that goal, but your consequential contribution to a particular person does. Thus, the reason offered in favor of joining this effort—to protect your fellow townspeople—is the very reason not to join the effort and do something more productive instead. Similarly, the moral aims one might seek to advance through political participation—reducing poverty, preserving the environment, providing health care, and so on—are usually better served by not participating in politics and taking direct action instead.

THE PROBLEMS IN PRACTICE

A further worry about trying to justify a duty of political participation on grounds of reciprocity arises when we look at real-world political behavior. When citizens participate in politics, it is not at all clear that their participation is aimed at universally desirable goods or shared purposes.

Consider a disanalogy between donating blood and participating in politics. It's obvious what someone who donates blood to a blood bank aims to accomplish—to help people who need blood get blood. But the aims of millions of political participants are vastly more diverse than that, and they frequently find themselves in conflict with each other. For instance, the political contributions of Democrats are not "aimed at the same purpose" as the contributions of Republicans. Perhaps we aim at the same purposes if we describe these purposes in a sufficiently general way—for instance, we all want a free and equal society. But participants' *specific* political visions vary dramatically. Does equality mean that everyone is taxed at an equal rate? Or does it mean that the rich should pay a higher rate to produce a more equal distribution of wealth and income? Along the same lines, we can all agree that safety is a universally desirable good. But what does this mean in concrete terms? A more active military? A *less* active military? Gun prohibition? Expanded access to guns? The death penalty? It strikes me as unlikely that a Democrat who votes for stricter gun control with the intention of increasing public safety will see the Republican's vote *against* stricter gun control (also with the intention of increasing public safety) as an appropriate return for their political contribution.

To reinforce my doubts about the "fitting return" defense of political participation, consider the following. If you're a Democrat, ask yourself if a neighbor's vote for a Republican was a fitting return for your vote. If you're a Republican, ask yourself if a neighbor's vote for a Democrat was a fitting return for your vote. My suspicion is that your answer is "no." To that point, notice how unrealistic the following conversation sounds:

Democrat: So, did you do your duty and turn out to vote yesterday?

Republican: I sure did!

Democrat: Great! If you don't mind, may I ask whom you voted for?

Republican: The Republican candidate, of course—I wanted to lower taxes, strengthen gun rights, and tighten abortion restrictions.

Democrat: Thanks—I owe you one!

That this dialogue is the stuff of pure fiction suggests that few truly believe that *mere* participation in the political process is a fitting return for one's own participation. Most Democrats would probably prefer that Republicans not participate at all and vice versa.

Moreover, to have a fairness-based duty to accept the burdens of contributing to some good, it's not enough that others simply contribute; they have to contribute in the right way.[36] Consider once more John and the community walkways. Let's stipulate that John is under a moral obligation to contribute in some form if (nearly) everyone in his neighborhood is pitching in to clean up their shared walkways. But imagine half of the neighborhood isn't joining in the effort; they're happy to lounge at the pool instead of collecting trash. Many of those who *are* working on the walkways aren't doing a careful job—it turns out that they are actually just shuffling the clutter around, leaving the walkways no clearer than they were before. Some of them are even littering during the cleanup, making the problem worse. In short, the neighbors do a poor job of providing the good in question. In this case, John is under no moral obligation to spend his Saturday on the unproductive cleanup effort. Many of his neighbors aren't making any sort of contribution at all and many of the contributors aren't making the right *sort* of contribution.

Our political situation is close enough to this case to raise doubts about a duty of political participation in the real world, even if (contrary to my earlier arguments) we have such a duty in the idealized conditions considered by some democratic theorists. To start, many Americans don't participate in politics at all. For instance, somewhere between 40% and 60% of eligible Americans don't cast a vote, depending on the election.[37] The rates of other forms of political participation, such as working for a candidate or donating to a campaign, are even lower.[38]

Moreover, as I discussed in earlier chapters, a good deal of political participation is ill-informed and biased. I won't rehash the evidence, but I will remind you of the remark from political scientist Larry Bartels: "The political ignorance of the American voter is one of the best-documented features of contemporary politics."[39] Citizens who are highly engaged in politics are "the most deeply partisan and ideological."[40] More knowledgeable voters tend to assess new information with greater bias.[41] As we've seen, partisan bias impairs our capacity to use information to arrive at accurate beliefs. Ill-informed and biased participants can undermine the functioning of democratic governance because they do not hold policymakers accountable for bad decisions.

ENVIRONMENTAL GOODS: A CASE STUDY

Here's the key point: advocates of the reciprocity argument for a duty to participate cannot simply take it for granted that participants actually *are* providing the relevant sorts of political goods. To illustrate, let's take a closer look at one of the "universally desirable goods" mentioned by Brown—a clean environment. It is, at a minimum, up for debate whether American citizens have done an effective job of keeping their government accountable for providing this good. The country's carbon emissions have not been cut to a significant extent.[42] The U.S. government has a long track record of climate change inaction.[43] For instance, it has withdrawn from the Paris Agreement, an international effort aimed at preventing climate change—but even this agreement carries no penalties for failures to meet the targets.[44]

So why haven't political participants done their part to provide the universally desirable good of a clean environment? To start, it's worth emphasizing that it's not enough for citizens to engage in political action that *expresses* concern about climate change; the action must be informed by accurate beliefs about, for instance, the content of the relevant environmental legislation, effective methods of decarbonization, and so on. But as economist Bryan Caplan writes, "Good intentions are ubiquitous to politics; what is scarce is accurate beliefs."[45] Only 24% of Americans, for instance, know that cap-and-trade legislation—one prominent option for reducing emissions—addresses environmental issues.[46]

Moreover, the public's processing of environmental information is susceptible to politically motivated reasoning. The right is prone to politically motivated skepticism of climate change; the left is prone to politically motivated skepticism of nuclear power.[47] Thus, one side is resistant to recognizing the problem; the other side is resistant to recognizing what could be an effective solution to the problem.[48] To be clear, my aim here is not to assert that increased adoption of nuclear energy is an appropriate response to climate change (although I will note that scientists are far more bullish on nuclear energy than the general public), but rather to spotlight the bipartisan risk of closed-mindedness in public deliberation about climate change.[49] Partisans on both sides are forming environmental beliefs, not to achieve accuracy, but to align themselves with their political team.[50]

What explains the widespread ignorance and partisanship about environmental issues? The answer takes us back to the (in)effectiveness of political participation. Even if you *do* put in the work to form accurate beliefs about climate change and how to mitigate it, you typically cannot do anything useful with those beliefs. Your research might help you aim your advocacy at the best policy response to climate change, but your advocacy almost certainly won't change environmental policy for the better. As a result, in Caplan's terms, uninformed and highly partisan citizens are "rationally irrational."[51] There's little point in trying to form more accurate beliefs about politics, so you might as well indulge yourself and defend your political team.[52]

Here's an analogy. I'm inclined to accept the unpopular belief that Wilt Chamberlain is the greatest basketball player of all time. Now, Wilt happened to play on the Philadelphia 76ers—my favorite team. So am I biased in my evaluation? Almost certainly. (I've noticed that his numbers become less transcendent when you adjust for his era's pace of play.) But is it worth the time and discomfort of uprooting my bias and grappling with the evidence that suggests I'm wrong? No. Having accurate but unsettling beliefs about my favorite players doesn't do me any good. It's not like I have any control over the rosters of my favorite teams. The "rationally irrational" thing for me to do is to resist challenges to my satisfying-but-suspect beliefs about basketball.

Similarly, having accurate but unsettling political beliefs doesn't do individual citizens any good. As Dan Kahan writes,

> What an ordinary citizen believes about the effect of private gun possession, the contribution of humans to climate change, and like facts will typically have no meaningful impact on the risks these states of affairs pose or on adoption of policies relating to them. The reliable activation of affective stances that convey group allegiance will be the only use most citizens have for such beliefs. In such circumstances, politically motivated reasoning can be understood to be perfectly rational.[53]

Affirming their identity as a member of their political team is usually the only benefit citizens can gain from political participation and so that's what they seek.[54] The problem is, poorly informed and highly partisan participants won't hold legislators accountable for, for instance, their failure to effectively address climate change.[55] Many of the participants don't know what the legislators are doing or what the relevant policy options involve; those that do know tend to judge policies based on their partisan affiliation rather than their substance and effectiveness. Thus, there is little incentive for legislators to undertake meaningful action on climate change.

Here's the takeaway: if you have a duty to contribute to the production of, for instance, effective climate policy, it is probably not grounded in a debt that you owe to your fellow citizens for their contribution. Most of your fellow citizens are simply not making a contribution to the production of effective climate policy. Even if reciprocity-based arguments for a duty of political participation withstand my philosophical objections, they don't apply to our real-world political situation.

MOTIVATION MATTERS

Even when citizens contribute to good governance, you may not owe them a return. The intention of political participation is morally relevant. Remember, in the words of Christopher Achen and Larry Bartels, "Voters, even the most informed voters, typically make choices not on the basis of policy preferences or ideology, but on the basis of who they are—their social identities."[56] Suppose, then, that someone votes to express and affirm their social identity and ends up supporting a genuinely good policy. Does this vote generate a duty of reciprocity? I doubt it. By analogy, when a Second Amendment enthusiast waves her Gadsden flag at a rally to signal her preference not to be tread upon, the flag might produce a nice breeze for passersby. But those passersby don't owe her anything; her intention was not to cool them down but to cheer on her side.

My argument here echoes the earlier argument that we shouldn't receive moral credit for the economic benefits we provide for others as mere by-products of self-interested actions. Sure, Jeff Bezos has made millions of products more affordable, but his concern is to make money. By the same reasoning, people who vote and lobby for policies that benefit society should not receive moral credit when they are motivated by social identity expression rather than moral principle.

The motivation of many political participants might be even worse than benign social identity expression. Political scientists Shanto Iyengar and Masha Krupenkin write that "as animosity toward the opposing party has intensified, it has taken on a new role as the prime motivator in partisans' political lives."[57] They continue,

> The strengthening of partisan identity and affect has altered the psychological rewards that prompt partisans to become politically active. The primal sense of "us against them" makes partisans fixate on the goal of defeating and even humiliating the opposition at all costs.[58]

Surely I don't owe someone a return for their political participation when it's motivated by a desire to defeat and humiliate the opposition, even if their political participation coincidentally aligns with the principles of good governance.[59]

THE CASE FOR MORALLY COMMENDABLE FREE RIDING

Before moving on, I'll note that we can easily get carried away with free riding arguments. Free riding can be morally permissible or even commendable if you use your spared time and resources to provide urgent help to particular individuals.

Suppose you're on your way to buy some refreshments for a community picnic when you come across a child bitten by a snake. You drive her to the hospital for a lifesaving dose of antivenom instead of pitching in with picnic preparation. When you arrive at the picnic later and sip the lemonade you did not purchase, your neighbors will probably not begrudge your consumption. ("Sorry I wasn't able to help prepare the picnic—I was busy taking the Jones kid to the hospital." "Free loader! And the Jones kid isn't even from our neighborhood!")

In this case, you make neither a direct nor indirect contribution to the picnic and the beneficiary of your action is not a member of the relevant community. Still, I submit that it would be unreasonable for your neighbors to admonish you for free riding, given the magnitude of the benefit you produced for the snakebite victim and the comparative insignificance of your (forgone) contribution to the picnic. Similarly, if you decide to disengage from politics entirely and use your spared time to earn extra income to donate to the Against Malaria Foundation to save the lives of children in Ghana, you make neither direct nor indirect contributions to the good governance of your nation and the beneficiaries of your actions are not members of your national political community. Nevertheless, your decision is, at minimum, morally blameless and probably morally praiseworthy. (Even if you remain convinced that there is a fairness-based duty of political participation, you could still agree that this duty is *outweighed* by one's duty to meet urgent needs when you are in a position to do so at a reasonable cost to yourself.[60])

A final thought: you might naturally wonder how we should judge those political abstainers who do not make nonpolitical contributions. Aren't they in the wrong? They are—but they are in the wrong because they do nothing to contribute to a better world, not because they do nothing *political* to contribute to a better world.

Five

> Ours is not the task of fixing the entire world all at once, but of stretching out to mend the part of the world that is within our reach.
>
> —Clarissa Pinkola Estés (2003)

Perhaps the fairness argument gets things backwards. We're obligated to get involved in politics, not because of the goods provided by the state, but because of the *bads* provided by the state. Since we live in an unjust world, political theorist Eric Beerbohm argues that it's a mistake to

> locate our moral reason to participate in the unfairness we do to others when we take benefits from an enterprise in which we do not put in our share. History's great democratic reformers, who have confronted injustice publicly and eloquently, do not cite the state benefits they receive as their reason for engaging in political action. They have been concerned with the wrongs of the current regime.[1]

One strength of this approach is that it is consistent with the reality that many of your fellow citizens are engaging in politics poorly. It is precisely *because* your governing institutions are unjust that you have a duty to try to reform them.

INACTION AND COMPLICITY

Beerbohm's argument centers on the idea that citizens are complicit in the injustices committed by their government:

> The analysis behind this is not that I owe the unjust state anything in return, because it has benefited me. It is rather that I have been causally contributing to an unjust structure in an atomic but authentic way. I risk serving as an unwitting accessory. That I also benefit from the very injustices implicated in the system may further strengthen my positive obligations to aim for a reformed state.[2]

You bear moral responsibility for state injustice in virtue of contributing to state injustice.[3] And because you are responsible for state injustice, you are under a moral obligation to improve it. You helped make the mess, so you need to help clean it up.

Here's one initial complication with using the complicity argument to defend a duty of political participation: the argument is better directed at citizens who participate *poorly* rather than citizens who don't participate at all. Beerbohm identifies two major ways in which citizens contribute to political wrongdoing. First, citizens are "accessories to injustice" insofar as they "select lawmakers and sponsor the state exercise of power that produces political injustice."[4] If you vote or campaign for unjust laws and lawmakers, you bear some of the blame for the injustice they produce. Second, you are a "coprincipal" insofar as you "engage in a coordinated enterprise with lawmakers in aiming for unjustifiable basic structures."[5] Fossil fuel lobbyists who work with politicians to snuff out clean energy are morally responsible for the harms of the policy they fought to implement.

But if you sit out politics altogether, you neither select lawmakers nor coordinate with them. At first blush, then, it's hard to see why political abstainers bear moral responsibility for the injustices produced by their governments. However, this dismissal of responsibility would be too quick. After all, we can be held morally responsible for inaction as well as action. If a sadist announces they'll torture an innocent person unless you raise your hand, not raising your hand makes you complicit in the wrong done to the victim.[6]

IS POLITICS SPECIAL?

Still, more work remains for those who would invoke complicity to justify a duty of political participation. If you're complicit in all of the moral wrongs that you don't actively resist, then you are complicit in an endless series of wrongs. If you don't participate in efforts to eradicate malaria, then you're complicit in the deaths of children who suffer from malaria. If you don't volunteer to teach reading, you're complicit in illiteracy. If you don't volunteer at a soup kitchen, you're complicit in food insecurity. Julia Maskivker puts the objection this way:

> There are many collective activities that are potentially capable of helping society (e.g. rallies to beat cancer, rallies to beat AIDS, or rallies to beat domestic violence). . . . What is morally special about voting that makes it morally obligatory vis-a-vis other forms of contributing to society?[7]

What the advocate of political participation needs to show is that we do something *uniquely* wrong when we fail to resist political injustice.

Maskivker argues that politics is morally special because government policy is exceptionally impactful:

> Governments are distinguished from other entities and institutions because it is reasonable to assume that they have more power to affect people's life prospects by way of their capacity to enact, or block, far-reaching public and social policy. Thus, if we ought to act as good Samaritans and help the common good, it seems that partaking of the mechanism that makes governments elected is essential.[8]

Yet the mere fact that the government has a far-reaching impact on people's lives isn't enough to show that political inaction is morally worse than, say, philanthropic inaction. The government's ability to impact people's lives is only one part of the equation—another part is *your* ability to impact the government. If your participation has little chance of nudging the government to better serve the common good, then your participation doesn't effectively serve the common good.

Consider an analogy. Suppose there is an outbreak of a virus that will kill and immiserate billions. The virus "has more power to affect people's life prospects" than any other ill facing humanity. But you have no reasonable chance of producing a cure. You can therefore do more good by tending to the sick than working in the lab. I say you should tend to the sick. Similarly, you can usually expect to do more good through direct charitable action than political participation. Thus, you should perform direct charitable action.

Perhaps we are uniquely implicated in the state's injustice because we have a unique relationship with our governing institutions. As Beerbohm says, complicity arguments are specifically concerned with wrongs committed by others "when we have some contributory nexus to them."[9] Beerbohm does not deny that we have a general moral obligation to fight injustice and relieve suffering in other cases; rather the point is that we bear *special* moral responsibility when injustices implicate us as citizens.

How, then, might political abstainers "contribute" to political injustice? One possibility is that we "enable the state's activities through our regular taxpaying."[10] Funding bank robbers no doubt makes you complicit in the bank robbery. The trouble is, taxes are *compelled*. If the bank robbers stole your Chevy at gunpoint and used it as their getaway car, we wouldn't blame you for the robbery.

A more promising argument focuses on the ways in which citizens voluntarily accept benefits from the state. More specifically,

> we willingly accept the receipt of a great diversity of state benefits. My silent acceptance of its largess can function as support for the state—signaling that I think the government is worthy of a transactional relationship. . . . That I also benefit from the very injustices implicated in the system may further strengthen my positive obligations to aim for a reformed state.[11]

Let's break down this argument. First, we need to pinpoint the specific benefits whose acceptance makes us complicit in state injustice. There are some state-provided benefits that citizens do not "willingly accept," such as national defense. Americans have no choice but to receive the protection of the U.S. military. That my receipt of this state benefit was unavoidable casts doubt on my complicity in state action. By analogy, if I have no way to avoid hearing my neighbor play beautiful music on a guitar she stole, it seems implausible to accuse me of complicity in the theft.

There are other benefits that you could decline but only at a prohibitive cost to yourself. You could, for instance, refuse to call the police when your life is threatened or consume food whose production was affected by government policy. However, refusal to accept state benefits in these sorts of cases could leave you dead. If you're drowning and accept a life preserver from a passing ship, are you complicit in the wrongdoings of its captain? At the very least, this would be a controversial claim. It might be unreasonable to demand that people refuse benefits when the cost of doing so is sufficiently high.

But all is not lost for the complicity argument. It is likely that political abstainers willingly accept state benefits that they could refuse at a reasonable cost to themselves. They visit parks, zoos, and museums that receive government support. They watch PBS and listen to NPR. Let's grant that willingly accepting these sorts of state benefits makes us complicit in state injustice. Should we conclude, then, that our complicity in state injustice obligates us "to aim for a reformed state" via our thoughtful political participation?[12]

HOW TO ABSOLVE YOURSELF OF COMPLICITY IN INJUSTICE

My doubts at this stage of the complicity argument surround the idea that political action is the appropriate response to complicity in political injustice. For one, I've argued that our complicity is clearest when we willingly accept state benefits that we could refuse at a reasonable cost. But in these cases, the way to avoid complicity is not to "aim for a reformed state"— rather, it is to refuse the benefits in the first place.[13] If accepting a grant from the National Endowment for the Humanities makes you complicit in the injustices committed by the U.S. government, then you should not accept the grant. Refusal to partake of the benefits of unjust practices is our standard approach to avoiding complicity. If you buy a stolen TV out of a van, you're complicit in the theft—so don't buy the TV. Only a counterintuitive approach would permit you to buy the TV on the condition that afterwards you'll lobby the thief to change her criminal ways.

However, let's suppose, for argument's sake, that you do bear some moral responsibility for the actions of those who provide you with benefits even if you did not have a reasonable alternative to accepting those benefits. For instance, it seems normal to feel guilty if you learn that the public water supply from which you drink was unjustly seized by your local government. The costs of refusing to use public water might be prohibitively high, but you would naturally want to make amends to those treated wrongly by your political institutions.

Thus, we arrive at the core question: if you find yourself complicit in state injustice, is distinctively political action required to make amends? At a minimum, it is morally permissible to make amends through nonpolitical action—that is, by directly remedying the harms done to the victims of the injustice rather than aiming to reform the root cause of the injustice. Indeed, I would go further and say that political action that does not effectively serve a reparative purpose fails to honor your duty to the victims of injustice. The recommendation to "mend the part of the world that is in our reach" is not a call to ignore social injustice; rather, we should dedicate ourselves to addressing those wrongs that we actually have the power to make right.[14]

Let me motivate this idea with a case. Suppose a skilled hacker with impeccable taste in philosophy but questionable personal morals loves this book and decides to commit an ongoing injustice: skim a bit from innocent people's bank accounts and transfer the money to me each week. As I find myself in the thick of this injustice, I consider two ways of making it right. First, I could take a night course on computer programing to try to stop the wrongdoing at the source, but my odds of successfully thwarting the hacker are exceedingly low. Alternatively, I could directly address the harm done to the victims of the injustice. I could, for instance, track down those robbed by the hacker and return the money that was stolen from them. I contend that taking direct action to ameliorate the effects of the hacking is morally better than engaging in an unhelpful attempt to stop the hacking at its source. (If you asked the victims of the hacking what they would prefer, I imagine they would agree.)

The application of this principle to state injustice can take a wide variety of forms. Maybe you're a dentist who benefits from needlessly restrictive licensing requirements that drive up the cost of routine teeth cleaning. A good way to remedy this injustice would be to provide free dental care for low income families. Perhaps it's unfair that you don't pay a higher tax rate that could provide revenue for higher-quality education for children from economically disadvantaged households. To ameliorate this wrong, take your surplus income and donate to child literacy programs. Or, you could donate to programs overseas to offset the harm done by your government's unjust foreign policy.

Indeed, I'll make the stronger claim that you are not absolved of complicity in injustice when you take actions that "aim for a reformed state" but cannot reasonably be expected to benefit the victims of injustice. Suppose your town is at risk of flooding owing to a crack in a dam that you neglected to monitor. If you don't have the knowledge or material resources to repair the dam, then you ought not waste your time trying to repair it. Instead, you're obligated to take action to mitigate the impending disaster—for instance, by alerting the townspeople to the need to evacuate or helping those displaced by the flood rebuild their homes. To make amends for your complicity in injustice, you should take the most effective steps toward making the victims of injustice whole.

POLITICAL ABSTENTION AS PRIVILEGE

I'll end this chapter by addressing an argument against political abstention that is adjacent to the complicity objection. I sometimes hear this argument in conversation and it was nicely summarized in a blog post that made the rounds on social media:

> I want my friends to understand that "staying out of politics" or being "sick of politics" is privilege in action. Your privilege allows you to live a non-political existence. Your wealth, your race, your abilities or your gender allows you to live a life in which you likely will not be a target of bigotry, attacks, deportation, or genocide. You don't want to get political, you don't want to fight because your life and safety are not at stake.[15]

I think there is a good deal of truth in this statement. Politics tends to work out well for the privileged and badly for those who aren't so fortunate. However, should we conclude that the privileged have a duty to participate in politics because their privilege shields them from the adverse effects of politics? I don't think so.

Consider that it's a privilege to be in a position where I don't have to worry much about suffering from malaria. I was lucky to be born in a time and place where malaria simply isn't a concern. But what follows from that? Maybe we should conclude that those of us lucky enough to be unaffected by malaria should do what we can to help those who aren't so lucky (say, by donating to the Against Malaria Foundation). That conclusion sounds exactly right. So, along the same lines, those of us lucky enough to be unaffected by political injustice should help those who *are* affected. But individual political participation rarely does that. I have little hope of changing laws that needlessly worsen the job prospects of those who have served time in prison, but I can make a meaningful contribution to organizations that help them find work. That you are unaffected by political injustice does not imply that you're obligated to take distinctively political means to combatting injustice.

Perhaps, though, I am overlooking an important dimension of political participation. Sometimes our actions are morally meaningful simply because of what they *say*. Along these lines, Beerbohm writes, "The very idea of complicity, I think, relies on a conception of action as having partly expressive or symbolic value that is morally distinct from its production value."[16] Maybe political inaction is wrong because it expresses a lack of concern for injustice and its victims. Let's turn to that question now.

Six

> If your main goal is to show that your heart is in the right place, then your heart is not in the right place.
>
> —David Schmidtz[1]

Ignoring politics doesn't cause harm or treat anyone unfairly. But there are things you shouldn't do even though they don't cause harm or treat anyone unfairly. If you intentionally sneeze on the quilt that's been in your family for three generations, it seems like you've done something wrong. The action sends a bad message—you don't have the proper respect for your family heirlooms.

Maybe political abstention is like this. Even though abstainers aren't hurting people or violating their rights, binge watching Netflix instead of protesting systemic injustice sends a bad message. In the words of philosopher Stanley Benn,

> Political activity may be a form of moral self-expression, necessary not for achieving any objective beyond itself (for the cause may be lost), nor yet for the satisfaction of knowing that one had let everyone else know that one was on the side of the right, but because one could not seriously claim, even to oneself, to be on that side without expressing the attitude by the actions most appropriate to it in the paradigm case.[2]

So, the thought goes, you have an *expressive* duty to participate in politics.

This chapter explores several arguments for an expressive duty of political participation. These arguments are unpersuasive for a variety of reasons. For one, the case for an expressive duty tends to lose its luster when we know that the expression is unlikely to do much good. Moreover, if our duty to participate is purely expressive, then we can honor this duty with bumper stickers instead of votes—a result that will no doubt leave advocates of political engagement unsatisfied. I also draw attention to a potential paradox: engaging in behavior to express your concern for justice instead of engaging in behavior that more effectively *promotes* justice may, ironically, send the wrong moral message.

THE EXPRESSIVE ARGUMENT

As a general point, it seems as though the expressive significance of actions can have moral significance. Suppose there is an enormous crowd at an event honoring Nobel Prize winner Norman Borlaug, an agronomist whose work saved the lives of millions.[3] As Borlaug is introduced, the crowd emits deafening applause. However, you notice an attendee sitting on his hands, refusing to clap. Although this individual's refusal to clap makes no noticeable difference to the reception Borlaug receives, he sends a morally blameworthy message. Political abstention might be similarly blameworthy.

Philosophers Loren Lomasky and Geoffrey Brennan summarize the expressive argument for political participation thusly:

> Abstention by itself is not bad faith. It is, though, arguably discreditable. The office of citizen is no mean one,

and to fail to display adequate regard for the station can be categorized as inherently condemnable. Not voting, so construed, is akin to declining to stand at the playing of the national anthem or trampling on the flag. Each is an expressively laden action that aligns one with certain political values and against others. Therefore, they are properly subject to praise or blame in virtue of what they *mean*, not simply because of what they *bring about*.[4]

According to this argument, an individual's choice to ignore politics, like an individual's refusal to clap for a great humanitarian, has expressive significance despite having little consequential significance. Ignoring politics sends the message that your concern for causes like justice and the relief of suffering is inadequate.

My case against the expressive argument for political participation begins by distinguishing between the possession of an attitude and the expression of an attitude. Clearly, any decent person will have certain attitudes toward injustice. They may rise to anger when they witness someone being treated unjustly. They will empathize with the victims of injustice. They will have the desire to reduce injustice. However, it does not follow from the claim that decent people will have certain attitudes toward injustice that they are morally obligated to engage in political behavior that *expresses* those attitudes.

To motivate my skepticism about duties to perform purely expressive actions, consider an analogy:

> An asteroid is set to strike your town. It will kill, injure, and impoverish people. You have the opportunity to toss a penny in a fountain and audibly wish for the asteroid to break up and scatter harmlessly into the ocean. You don't make the wish.

Any decent person will have a negative attitude toward the effects of the asteroid. They would prefer that it not strike, of course. They will empathize with those harmed by the asteroid. What's more, wishing for the asteroid to veer off harmlessly *expresses* these attitudes. But, crucially, making the wish wouldn't actually *affect* the asteroid. For this reason, it is morally permissible to not make the wish. (If you're tempted to disagree, ask yourself if you feel guilty for never having wished for the miraculous disappearance of real-world natural disasters.)

To be clear, this argument doesn't imply that it's morally permissible to do *nothing* about the harms caused by the asteroid. You might be obligated to give food and shelter to asteroid victims or tend to the injured. However, this behavior is consequential, not (merely) expressive.

Just as the ineffectiveness of a purely expressive wish explains why you're under no obligation to make that wish, the ineffectiveness of a purely expressive political action explains why you're under no obligation to undertake that action. Of course, you may have an obligation to relieve the suffering caused by injustice just as you may have an obligation to relieve the suffering caused by the asteroid. But here again, the obligation is to perform consequential behavior—that is, behavior that *actually* relieves suffering and combats injustice rather than behavior that merely signals that you care about suffering and injustice.

PRIVATE AND PUBLIC EXPRESSION

A further problem for the expressive argument is that much of people's political participation takes place in private. As Lomasky and Brennan note, "Because the ballot is secret, the direction of one's vote is not subject to scrutiny and thus lacks the expressive dimensions of a genuinely public performance."[5] When you clap for the humanitarian, your action publicly expresses your support. But no one would accuse you of wrongdoing if you don't clap for him while you're watching the event by yourself on television. If our duty is to perform a public act of political expression, then people who vote and donate to campaigns in private aren't doing their duty. However, this result seems contrary to how most people conceive of a duty of political participation—our obligation is to participate, not to be *seen* participating.

Suppose, though, that you accept this line of argument and accept that we *do* have a duty to engage in public political expression. Consider the strange implications that would follow. It seems, for instance, that a duty to publicly engage in political expression implies that we have at least some moral obligation to slap political bumper stickers on our car. Sure, no one has ever been swayed by a bumper sticker, but that's not what matters—sending the signal is what matters.[6] Similarly, you'd be bound by moral duty to post selfies with your "I Voted" sticker to social media on Election Day. That is, you'd be morally blameworthy for not doing so. This result is implausible.

Indeed, the moral distinction between genuine political activism and so-called "slacktivism" would collapse if the whole of our obligation to participate in politics were expressive. "Slacktivism" is a term coined to describe low-effort, low-impact political action like giving a "thumbs up" to a Facebook post publicizing a cause. I doubt anyone would seriously propose that you're morally obligated to post an angry or sad emoji whenever one of your friends shares a story about the latest injustice committed by the government. But if our duty to be politically active is expressive, it's hard to see why you *aren't* obligated to perform this sort of action.[7]

We can take this point a step further: many are of the opinion that engaging in low-effort political signaling is downright *bad*. The United Nations suggests that the very term "slacktivism" assumes that "people who support a cause by performing simple measures are not truly engaged or devoted to making a change."[8] I take it that people's criticism of slacktivism rests on the thought that if someone *really* cared about the cause, they'd do something that effectively advances the cause instead of simply publicizing their concern for the cause. (Indeed, my guess is that those who endorse a duty to participate would disapprove upon hearing that their friend voted *only* so that she would get an "I Voted" sticker to wear.) If you truly care about feeding the hungry, then you should feed the hungry—and you can leave your "Feed the Hungry" T-shirt at home.

To reinforce this point, suppose that you've fallen ill and need some help getting meals, going to medical appointments, and so on. When your friend Arthur learns of your condition, he volunteers to bring you dinner and drive you to your doctor. When your friend Beth learns of your condition, she merely says, "My thoughts are with you during this trying time." Arthur's expression of concern for your well-being seems more sincere precisely because it makes a difference to your well-being.[9]

Before moving on, let me briefly note that the case for an expressive duty to participate runs afoul of the problem of specifying what makes politics morally unique. More specifically, why do we have a special duty to express our political attitudes but not our attitudes about other weighty moral concerns? Intuitively, it doesn't seem as though we have a duty to express our attitudes about preventing malaria-related deaths by "liking" a Facebook post from the Against Malaria Foundation. We don't blame people who forgo moralizing bumper stickers. (What, you don't have a "Coexist" sticker on your bumper? Are you saying that you *don't* want us to coexist?) I see no reason to treat political expression any differently.

THE MESSAGE OF MERE PARTICIPATION

Perhaps, despite my efforts so far, you still that think there is an expressive duty to participate in politics. An important question remains: what, exactly, do we need to do to express the right message? Does *mere* participation do the job?

Those who believe in an expressive duty to participate in politics are unlikely to be satisfied by just any old form of participation. Presumably, you only send the right message if you participate in politics *well*. At a minimum, this would mean satisfying certain procedural standards. It might not matter whether you end up voting for a Democrat or a Republican, but you at least need to put in some effort. If you participate thoughtlessly by voting for the candidate who makes the most offensive jokes in the debates, you send a bad message— namely, that you need not aim your political participation at what is just (or at least, what you have good reason for thinking is just). As Lomasky and Brennan write, "The mere act of showing up at the polls every several years and grabbing some levers is palpably inadequate to qualify as a significant act of political expression."[10]

Indeed, thoughtless acts of political expression might be positively blameworthy. If you participate simply to prop up your self-image as a compassionate cosmopolitan or a tough-but-fair realist, giving no thought to whether your favored policies and politicians are good ones, then the message your participation sends is one of self-indulgence. Once, when I told my students that I don't vote, one of them said, "With all due respect, professor, not voting is *selfish*." (Although I disagreed with his argument, I respected the student's chutzpah in calling me out.) But political participation itself can be selfish if your motivation is nothing more than low-cost partisan signaling. And, as we've seen, evidence indicates that this is precisely the motivation for many participants. So, it turns out that many politically active people aren't fulfilling their purported expressive duty.

Of course, this implication isn't a deal breaker for the view that there is an expressive duty to participate. Perhaps it simply turns out that most of us aren't fully honoring our expressive duty. On its own, then, my argument would only show that we have to participate well. That is, our expressive duty obligates us to prepare in the sorts of ways discussed in earlier chapters: acquire political information, study philosophy and the social sciences, and do our best to debias ourselves. But what's the harm in that? Why *not* engage in labor-intensive participation?

Here's one reason: labor-intensive participation comes at a higher opportunity cost. That is, it siphons additional time and energy away from other, more beneficial activities. Thus, you'd be losing the chance to make the world a better place simply to send the right signal.

This last point speaks to an irony in expressive arguments for participation: forgoing the opportunity to help people to send the signal that you care about helping people actually sends the *wrong* signal. *Helping* people is the right way to send the signal that you care about helping people. Think back to the asteroid case. Your very act of helping those harmed by the asteroid expresses your attitude about the harms of the asteroid. Consider how bizarre it would be for someone to say, "I know you've given shelter to those displaced by the asteroid, but you still need to show me you *care* about the asteroid's destruction." You fulfill whatever expressive duty you might have by taking consequential action.

Turning back to politics, maybe you think that the government has done a bad job addressing the problem of food insecurity. Taking direct action such as volunteering at or donating to a food bank sends the signal that you care about the unresolved problem of food insecurity more effectively than casting a purely expressive vote for the candidate you think is the best on the issue.

Along these lines, consider a case that makes the choice between consequential action and expressive action particularly vivid. You pass a starving child on the street who asks you for money to buy food. You have some money but you're reluctant to hand it over. Why? Well, it happens that you were on your way to buy a shirt that reads "Feed the Hungry" and you don't have enough money for the shirt and the child. Surely letting the child go hungry so that you can afford the T-shirt sends the wrong message (to say nothing of the moral wrong you would commit by allowing easily preventable harm to come to the child). To paraphrase philosopher David Schmidtz, if your aim is to simply broadcast that you have good intentions, then you don't have good intentions.[11]

PARTICIPATION AS AN EXPRESSION OF GRATITUDE

Another variation on the expressive argument claims that you should participate in politics to honor the sacrifices of those who fought to secure your right to participate. Political participation, then, is an expression of gratitude. Just as it would be ungrateful for you to toss aside a gift that your sister spent months crafting for you, it is ungrateful for you to toss aside the opportunity to exercise the democratic rights that so many sacrificed for.

One initial worry about this argument is that it's simply not clear to what extent the fight for democratic rights has been motivated by a belief in the *freedom* to participate rather than a *duty* to participate. Consider again the controversy over Colin Kaepernick's refusal to stand for the national anthem. A number of veterans have defended these protests despite disagreeing with the message. They argue that they fought for the freedom to exercise one's rights as one sees fit. Kelly Rodriguez, an Army medic veteran, puts it this way:

> I'm supporting and defending the Constitution of the United States. . . . People have tons of opinions I completely disagree with, but that's what makes America great. We're safer. We have tons of opinions, many different beliefs. That's what makes our culture so unique, and what I serve.[12]

Indeed, Rodriguez explicitly says that she does not "feel disrespected" by the protests.[13] Of course, other veterans feel differently. But this difference of opinion speaks to the difficulty of basing a duty to participate in politics on sweeping claims about how to appropriately honor those who sacrificed for the right to participate.

More generally, the mere fact that many people sacrificed so that you could do something doesn't imply that you are obligated to do that thing. For instance, people have fought to win and preserve the freedom of the press, but their sacrifices don't obligate you to start a newspaper.[14] Plenty of dedicated citizens have worked hard to legalize marijuana. But you aren't morally obligated to smoke marijuana to honor their hard work. Why not? Because your obligation to exercise a given right depends on the nature of the right itself and not the history of how you came to possess that right. That Ad-Rock, MCA, and Mike D fought for your right to party doesn't obligate you to party; you'd need an independent moral reason to party.

Moreover, you can show your gratitude for someone's sacrifices in ways other than doing the thing they themselves sacrificed for. Consider Ruth Bader Ginsburg's trailblazing work as a woman in law. (When Ginsburg attended Harvard Law School she was one of nine women in a class of 500; upon their arrival, the Dean asked them, "How do you justify taking a spot from a qualified man?")[15] Filmmaker Mimi Leder decided to honor Ginsburg by making a movie about her life.[16] Although Ginsburg helped pave the way for women in law, Leder's expression of gratitude did not take the form of practicing the law herself; however, the expression was still perfectly fitting. Similarly, you can honor the sacrifices of those who fought for democratic freedoms in ways that do not involve political participation, such as writing a heartfelt op-ed.

IS POLITICAL ACTIVISM VIRTUOUS?

Sometimes philosophers appeal to considerations of virtue to explain why certain behaviors are praiseworthy even when they don't produce the best consequences or honor a moral duty.[17] Your actions express your character. So perhaps deliberately sneezing on the family quilt is wrong because a person of good moral character simply wouldn't do that sort of thing. Similarly, political activism might be the right thing to do because it's the sort of thing that a virtuous person would do.

Virtue ethicist Rosalind Hursthouse stresses a point made by Aristotle: our moral evaluations of human beings are not all that different from the nonmoral evaluations we make of things like knives or lions.[18] (Indeed, we sometimes say things like, "This knife has many virtues: it's cheap, sharp, and durable.") The "virtues" or excellences of lions are those traits that enable them to flourish in the ways characteristic of lions—to hunt, care for their offspring, and so on. The virtues of a lion are different than the virtues of an oak tree, whose flourishing takes on an entirely different form. And so it goes with humans. The virtues of humans are those character traits that enable us to flourish in the ways characteristic of humans. Virtuous character traits might include those that help us to stay in good health, enjoy pleasure and avoid pain, do right by future generations of humans, facilitate social cooperation, and so on.[19]

By way of example, Hursthouse counts charity as a virtue because "it serves the good functioning of the social group by fostering the individual survival, freedom from pain, and enjoyment of its members, and also by fostering its cohesion."[20] She continues with a sketch of some other virtues:

> Without honesty, generosity, and loyalty we would miss out on one of our greatest sources of characteristic enjoyment, namely loving relationships; without honesty we would be unable to cooperate or to acquire knowledge and pass it on to the next generation to build on. And it has long been a commonplace that justice and fidelity to promises enable us to function as a social, cooperating group.[21]

Assuming for argument's sake that something like this conception of virtue is on the right track, should we conclude that a virtuous person will be politically active?[22] The most promising route to this conclusion will begin with Hursthouse's claim that virtues serve "the good functioning of the social group."[23] In particular, she singles out justice as a trait that enables "us to function as a social, cooperating group."[24] Thus, you might reasonably think that a person who possesses the virtue of justice will engage in political activities that facilitate social cooperation.

In response, let me first note that nothing in this understanding of justice restricts us to distinctively political contributions to the good functioning of the social group. Virtue ethicists recognize that the same virtue can manifest itself in different ways.[25] The soldier who risks her life in battle exhibits courage but so does the employee who refuses to follow his boss's orders to defraud a customer.

Justice is no different. You act justly when you ensure that your company's process for evaluating job applicants is fair, when you help someone who was wrongly imprisoned get back on their feet, and so on. Justice need not manifest itself in the voting booth just as courage need not manifest itself on the battlefield.[26]

I'll even go out on a limb and suggest that the virtuous person actively ignores politics in favor of other pursuits. Virtue ethicists agree that the virtuous person acts with "practical wisdom." Philosopher Neera Badhwar writes, "A virtuous person is practically wise. . . . She knows which ends are worth striving for, how to prioritize them, and how best to achieve them."[27] Along similar lines, virtue ethicist Philippa Foot says: "Wisdom, as I see it, has two parts. In the first place, the wise man knows the means to certain good ends; and secondly he knows how much particular ends are worth."[28] A wise person will not spend her time collecting lint because that particular end isn't worthwhile. Nor would a wise person use healing crystals because that decision would indicate that she doesn't know effective *means* to the good end of health. It is this latter point—that the wise person knows and takes effective means to good ends—that matters here. A wise citizen has good ends like benevolence and justice but knows that political participation is not usually an effective means to those ends. So practical wisdom dictates that we pursue justice via nonpolitical means that *are* effective, just as it dictates that we pursue health via diet, exercise, and medicine rather than healing crystals.

Here's a final thought on virtue and political participation. In the food insecurity case I proposed above, it is perfectly clear that letting a child go hungry so you can buy a T-shirt reading "Feed the Hungry" is not something a virtuous person would do. Forgoing the opportunity to feed the hungry to publicize your concern for feeding the hungry is hardly expressive of virtue. So I don't see why casting a purely expressive vote at the expense of a chance to take effective action is something virtuous people would do either.

BUT CAN YOU STILL COMPLAIN?

The last objection I'll consider alleges that you can't complain about politics if you don't participate. I take this objection particularly seriously. Why? Because, as my friends, family, coworkers, department chair, students, head of human resources, office manager, neighbors, mail carrier, barber, editor, doctor, veterinarian, day care providers, Uber drivers, flight attendants, and baristas will tell you, the right to complain is something I hold sacred.

At first blush, it looks like the ineffectiveness of political action enables us to quickly rebut this argument. You lose the right to complain about an outcome when you had the opportunity to change that outcome but chose not to. However, you have the right to complain about bad or unfair outcomes over which you have no control. Since your political participation does not typically empower you to exert control over political outcomes, you need not participate in politics to complain about politics.

By way of support, imagine the following conversation with your school's cafeteria server:

Server: We have a strict policy of only serving Pepsi.

You: Ugh, I don't like Pepsi.

Server: Hey, if you don't order something different, you can't complain.

You: OK, so can I have a Coke?

Server: No. Didn't you hear what I said? We only serve Pepsi. But at least you can complain now.

Needless to say, this would be a bizarre conversation. Whether you have grounds for complaining about the immutable Pepsi-only policy is independent of whether you make the pointless attempt to order a Coke instead. You may complain simply on the grounds that the policy is a bad one.

Now, if the server offered you a Coke but you ordered Pepsi instead, then you'd lose the right to complain about drinking Pepsi. In this case, you have it within your power to change the outcome (at a reasonable cost to yourself, and so on). But you generally do not have it within your power to change political outcomes. Thus, you may complain about politicians and policies simply on the grounds that they are bad ones.

However, a stronger version of this objection is available: complaining while abstaining borders on a kind of hypocrisy.[29] On the one hand, your (in)action expresses the attitude that politics doesn't matter or isn't worth your time; on the other hand, your complaint expresses the attitude that it *does* matter and *is* worth your time.

My reply to this line of reasoning makes use of the arguments that I've already put on the table. You can abstain from politics without thinking that politics is unimportant. You might abstain from politics because you doubt that your participation is an effective means of combating injustice just as you might abstain from wishing for the asteroid to change course because you doubt that wishing is an effective means of changing the asteroid's course. We wouldn't infer that the "wish abstainer" thereby believes that the asteroid is unimportant and thus loses her right to bemoan the harms caused by the asteroid. Similarly, we shouldn't assume that the political abstainer believes that politics is unimportant and thus loses her right to bemoan the harms caused by politics. Indeed, taking direct action to ameliorate the harms caused or allowed by bad governance signals your attitude that politics matters. So even political abstainers should feel free to air their grievances about the political system.

Seven

> You have it in your power to form no opinion about this or that,
> and so to have peace of mind.
>
> —Marcus Aurelius, *Meditations*

Here's something dumb I do every year. At some point during October in Virginia, the weather cools down enough that I switch the thermostat from air conditioning to heating. But inevitably we run into a spell of hot weather that lasts a few days. How do I respond? *I literally get mad at the weather*. I stare at the thermostat and fume at the prospect of flipping it back to air conditioning. In other words, I resent having to move my finger an inch because I feel as though I have been wronged by the weather—it's *unfair* that it would be hot in October. (I told you it was dumb.)

Why am I mentioning this? Because it illustrates the irrationality of getting angry over something you can't change. I can't change the weather. However, I can adjust my own behavior in response to the weather. It makes no sense to seethe at the heat spell—I can switch on the AC and move on with my life.

You should do the same with politics. You and I cannot change the country's political situation. However, we can adjust our own behavior in response to its political situation.

It's pointless to rage at politicians and pundits because you think they're wrong about how to alleviate poverty. Maybe they *are* wrong, but there's nothing you can do about it. Instead, you can focus on what you *can* control; you could, for instance, do your part to alleviate poverty by working overtime and donating your extra earnings to an effective charity.

So far, I've argued that you are under no moral obligation to participate in politics. Now I'll explore some of the therapeutic benefits of ignoring politics: it's good for you, your relationships, and society as a whole.

POLITICS MAKES US MISERABLE

The philosopher John Rawls writes of the typical citizen in a just society:

> The time and thought that he devotes to forming his [political] views is not governed by the likely material reward of political influence. Rather it is an activity enjoyable in itself that leads to a larger conception of society and to the development of his intellectual and moral faculties.[1]

Whatever the merits of Rawls's description of citizens in an ideal society, it doesn't seem to apply to citizens of our own society. Politics tends to make us miserable rather than being "enjoyable in itself."

One reason why staying politically informed can lower our happiness is that both news outlets and news consumers tend to focus on bad news instead of good news.[2] Ninety-five percent of adult Americans report regularly following the news— 82% check it every day—and over half of them say that it's a source of stress.[3]

I've always found it strange that people will dedicate hours of their day to watching and discussing the news only to be infuriated by it. Imagine if 95% of Americans reported regularly eating mushroom pizza—82% eating it at least once a day—but over half of them didn't like mushroom pizza. After working through your initial puzzlement at their behavior, I presume your advice to them would be simple: stop eating mushroom pizza. To quote my five-year-old son, "Why does Grandpa watch the news if he doesn't like the news?" (And in the interest of transparency, no, I don't always follow my own advice here. I'd say that's an indictment of me rather than my advice, though.)

Consider also that the psychological harm of "losing" in politics is greater than the psychological benefit of "winning." The loss of well-being experienced by partisans when their party loses is significantly larger than any well-being gain experienced by the winners.[4] And seeing one's side lose an election can have surprisingly devasting results. Immediately after their candidate lost the 2016 presidential election, the decline in life satisfaction experienced by Democrats was greater than the adverse effects of losing a job—a life event that has some of the worst effects on people's well-being.[5] Estimates based on recent survey data suggest that roughly 94 million Americans believe that politics has caused them stress, 44 million believe that it has cost them sleep, and 28 million believe that it has harmed their physical health.[6]

I suggest looking to the advice offered by the ancient Stoics for coping with fate. Philosophers Zeno and Chrysippus analogized the human condition to a dog tied to a cart:

> When a dog is tied to a cart, if it wants to follow it is pulled and follows, making its spontaneous act coincide

with necessity, but if it does not want to follow it will be compelled in any case. So it is with men too: even if they do not want to, they will be compelled in any case to follow what is destined.[7]

Political outcomes are, for all practical purposes, a matter of fate over which we as individuals have no control. We can either accept them and adjust our behavior accordingly, or we can pointlessly obsess over them to the detriment of our own well-being.

POLITICS SWALLOWS EVERYTHING

Here's something that worries me more than the stress of politics: our partisan commitments are beginning to swallow up the rest of our identity. Political scientist Lilliana Mason writes,

> A single vote can now indicate a person's partisan preference *as well as* his or her religion, race, ethnicity, gender, neighborhood, and favorite grocery store. This is no longer a single social identity. Partisanship can now be thought of as a mega-identity, with all the psychological and behavioral magnifications that implies.[8]

According to political scientists Shanto Iyengar and Sean Westwood, "The sense of partisan identification is all encompassing and affects behavior in both political and nonpolitical contexts."[9] You can use someone's vote to make a decent guess about their opinion of NASCAR, Whole Foods, and Lynyrd Skynyrd.

At first blush, the monopolization of our identity by our politics might not seem so bad. But consider that it homogenizes our social circles. Mason writes,

> At a dinner party today, talking about politics is increasingly also talking about religion and race. They are wrapped together in a new way. . . . Ironically, politics and religion may be increasingly acceptable topics at a dinner party today, because most of our dinner parties include mainly socially and politically similar people.[10]

This kind of sorting is increasing a sense of distance and competition between the opposing political sides. When people's other social identities align with their partisan identities, the members of one party drift further apart from members of the other party, and political conflict becomes more heated. By contrast, people with "cross-cutting" identities—that is, people whose partisan identities do *not* align with their other social identities in the standard pattern (picture a Prius-driving, Unitarian Republican who regularly attends vegan cooking classes)—are less hostile to out-party members and less likely to get angry about politics.[11] But as these "cross-cutters" grow scarce, politics gets bloodier.

To make matters worse, evidence indicates that "partisans' identities are increasingly anchored to hatred of the outparty rather than affection for their inparty."[12] We hate the other team more than we like our team. Why? We need to ramp up our animosity to the out party to rationalize our continued dedication to our own party despite its obvious shortcomings.[13] ("I know my party can be spineless and ineffective but I've got to stick with them because the other side is downright *evil*.") In brief, hatred of the out party is becoming increasingly central to our political identities as politics is becoming increasingly central to our identities as such.[14] I don't know about you, but I'd rather not be defined by stuff that

I hate—I don't want my life to revolve around inner ear infections and the Dallas Cowboys.

POLITICS IS BAD FOR YOUR RELATIONSHIPS

The philosopher John Stuart Mill says that "it is from political discussion, and collective political action, that one whose daily occupations concentrate his interests in a small circle round himself, learns to feel for and with his fellow-citizens, and becomes consciously a member of a great community."[15] Politics, on this view, expands our social circle and brings the community closer together. Unfortunately, evidence suggests the reverse: politics has the effect of tearing people apart. As Jason Brennan writes,

> Politics tends to make us hate each other, even when it shouldn't. . . . We tend to view political debate not as reasonable disputes about how to best achieve our shared aims but rather as a battle between the forces of light and darkness.[16]

In the most recent presidential election, 13% of Americans blocked friends on their social media accounts because of political disagreements.[17] Sixteen percent stopped talking to a friend or member of the family over politics; 13% ended a relationship with a friend or family member.[18] Over a quarter of Americans limited their "interactions with certain friends or family members" as a result of politics.[19] Nearly 30% of Americans consider it important to live where most people share their political opinions.[20]

Politics is now infiltrating our attitudes toward dating and marriage. People prefer to date co-partisans.[21] Over

60% of partisans want their children to marry within their own party (compared to about 30% in the late 1950s).[22] About one-half of Republicans and one-third of Democrats reported being "somewhat or very unhappy at the prospect of inter-party marriage."[23] Not only does it seem exhausting to police your relationships by politics, it can drive you away from friends and family (not to mention prospective friends and family).

Things look even worse when we move from personal relationships to the country as a whole. In the United States, it is becoming more common for partisans to see the other side as morally bad and worthy of blame and loathing.[24] Roughly half of Republicans believe that Democrats are "ignorant" and "spiteful," and similar numbers of Democrats think the same of Republicans.[25] About 40% of Democrats and Republicans believe that members of the other party "are not just worse for politics—they are downright evil."[26] Twenty percent of Democrats and 15% of Republicans agreed that "we'd be better off as a country if large numbers of" the opposing party "just died."[27] Think about that: politics is driving people to think that out-party deaths are a *good thing*.

When politics becomes partisan warfare, social trust and cohesion suffer.[28] In experimental settings, people are less trusting of out-party members and less generous toward them.[29] Employers are less likely to pursue job applicants whose resumes signal a partisan affiliation contrary to their own.[30] People are less likely to award a scholarship to an out-party member.[31] Consumers are more likely to buy from a politically like-minded seller.[32] As Iyengar and colleagues summarize, "Partisanship has bled into the non-political sphere, driving ordinary citizens to reward co-partisans and penalize opposing partisans."[33]

Particularly troubling is partisans' willingness to dehumanize those on the other side. Over half of partisans rated members of the opposing party as less evolved than members of their own party—they located out-party members farther away from an image of a modern human on a scale showing the stages of human evolution.[34] Another study presented partisans with a fake report accompanied by a photo of broken chairs and a description of a cookout where a fight had broken out, causing a rush to the exit and a number of injuries. When the event was affiliated with the Republican Party, Democratic subjects were more likely to agree that the event goers were "like animals"; a similar result was found for Republicans when told the gathering was Democratic.[35] A different study yielded a similar finding: about 20% of respondents believe that many members of the opposing party "lack the traits to be considered fully human—they behave like animals."[36] Dehumanization is a grave social problem: it can lead to discrimination, increased punitiveness, and violence.[37] Indeed, I'll note that 18% of Democrats and 13% of Republicans "feel violence would be justified" if the other party wins the 2020 presidential election.[38]

Although I've focused on the ways in which politics can make us unhappy and antisocial, it's worth noting that these findings also weaken the case for a moral duty to participate in politics.[39] Suppose there were a television show that made its viewers less generous, less sympathetic, and more violent toward those who think differently. It's safe to say that you'd have a moral obligation to avoid this television show unless you had a very powerful reason to watch it. Generally speaking, we have a moral obligation to avoid doing things that worsen our moral character and politics tends to do just that.

Only about a third of partisans think that members of the opposing party "have their heart in the right place but just come to different conclusions about what is best."[40] So here's an objection: we *should* disown out-party members because their politics expose their manifestly horrible character. You wouldn't keep Stalin on your Christmas card list, would you?

In reply, I'll first mention that our beliefs about people on the other side of the political aisle tend to be uninformed (a finding that should be unsurprising in light of the increasing social distance between the parties). Although people are misinformed about their own party, their misperceptions of the other side are worse.[41] For instance, Republicans estimate that over one-third of Democrats are atheist or agnostic, but the right number is under one-tenth.[42] Democrats think that 44% of Republicans earn at least $250,000 per year. The right number is 2.2%.[43]

On policy matters, we think that there are enormous differences between our views and the views of the other side. However, it turns out that the gap is smaller than we think—on issues like taxes and immigration, the *perceived* divide between Democrats and Republicans is larger than the actual divide.[44] You should at least have accurate beliefs about members of the other party before you disown them.

But what about those out-party members who do, in fact, endorse policies that you find morally objectionable? Surely *they* are ignorant, spiteful, or perhaps even evil people. How else could they err so badly?

This line of thought might be persuasive if the correct policy positions were obvious. In that case, people who hold incorrect views must be ignorant or evil. But it is simply not obvious what ought to be done about abortion, immigration, gun control, foreign aid, capital punishment, international trade, taxation, environmental regulation, criminal justice, military intervention, and many other policy matters. These are extremely complicated issues. Honest, well-meaning people can reach different conclusions about politics.

I'd also suggest that the ease with which we ascribe ignorance or evil to out-party members is a reflection of our own psychology rather than their moral character. We've seen how politically motivated reasoning causes us to selectively affirm information that flatters our side and condemns the opposition—it's no wonder, then, that our side seems clearly right and the other side seems clearly wrong. Moreover, as noted earlier, we justify our continued allegiance to our own side by amplifying the flaws of the other side, a tendency that could easily lead us to believe that members of the out party are malicious or stupid.[45]

As a general point, we think we are more moral and less biased than others.[46] So it is natural (although not justified) that we would believe that our own "perspective is the one that affords the greatest accuracy," causing us to "feel frustrated or even angry with those who dispute the authenticity and special insight" of our views.[47]

To reiterate a claim I made in an earlier chapter: I'm not endorsing the view that all political opinions have equal merit. There are opinions that are beyond the boundaries of what is reasonable or decent. (Don't be friends with Stalin.) I'm saying that we have grounds for thinking that many, if not most, of our political opponents are not downright evil. There *are* downright evil people in this world, but we should use caution when we apply this label. Someone can disagree with your politics and still be worthy of your business, your friendship, and your respect.

IN DEFENSE OF APOLITICAL POLITICS

Before moving on, I'd like to point out an irony: if politics weren't so central to our social identities, we'd probably get better politics. As social psychologist Jonathan Haidt says, "The more passionately we feel about something, the more likely it is that our reasoning is warped and unreliable."[48] When our partisan anger is stoked, we're less responsive to information and more prone to minimize risks.[49] Anger can also prompt "defense of convictions, solidarity with allies, and opposition to accommodation" and more politically motivated reasoning.[50] In brief, as politics absorbs more of our identity, political participants get more partisan, more hostile, and less willing to compromise.

Debates over whether to increase or decrease immigration restrictions (for example) would be more productive if they were more like debates over whether to use plastic or copper pipes and less like a holy war.[51] We don't feel as though our sense of self is under attack when someone challenges our plumbing choices. Plumbing is not at the core of (most of) our identities.

Of course, expecting people to bring the same clinical detachment to political decisions that they bring to plumbing decisions is a pipe dream. And that's understandable: there are weighty moral issues at stake in politics that aren't at stake in plumbing. But a world in which political debates were more clinical would be an improvement over the status quo. As things stand, partisans exert an outsized influence on our national politics. Those with the strongest political identities and strongest hostility to the other side are the most politically active.[52] We can do better. Politics need not be a Frankenstein's monster of religious zeal and sports fanaticism.

How could we move ourselves in that direction? It might be worth trying to tie your social identity to nonpolitical affiliations. (If these are cross-cutting identities, all the better.) Psychologists Jay Van Bavel and Andrea Pereira note, "When people are hungry for belonging, then they are more likely to adopt party beliefs unless they can find alternative means to satiate that goal."[53] You could start following your city's NBA team and cheer for basketball instead of politics. Better yet, quit your political party and join a local effective altruism group in your newly spared time.[54] If you insist on disregarding my advice to ignore politics, at least divorce your social identity from your politics. Your political participation will be better for it.

Conclusion

> If time be of all things the most precious, wasting time must
> be, as Poor Richard says, the greatest prodigality; since, as he
> elsewhere tells us, Lost time is never found again, and what we
> call time enough always proves little enough.
>
> —Benjamin Franklin

I've argued that political participation is, at most, morally
optional. There is no special obligation to be active in politics
any more than there is a special obligation to be active in the
arts. In closing, I'll go a step further: political participation
tends to be morally *wrong*.[1]

Let me introduce my argument with a case:

> Poppy elects to donate an hour of her day to making the
> world a better place. She has enough time to deliver either
> (i) a single kernel of popcorn to the local food bank or
> (ii) a four-month supply of life-saving medicine to a child
> across town.

I believe that Poppy is obligated to deliver the medicine instead
of the popcorn. To be clear: I take no stand on whether Poppy
is obligated to donate an hour of her time in the first place.
Rather, the thought is that if she donates that hour, *then* she is
obliged to put it to the (significantly) better use. A number of

philosophers have defended this sort of conditional obligation of effective altruism.[2]

Admittedly, this view looks strange at first blush. After all, how could it be morally permissible to give *no* help but morally impermissible to give *some* help? Upon reflection, though, this conclusion appears compelling.

To see why, let's first look at a scenario in which Poppy doesn't help at all:

> "Poppy, why don't you turn off the TV, get out of the house, and deliver that bottle of life-saving medicine?"
>
> "Eh, that's too much work."
>
> "Fair enough. Delivering the medicine would be a nice thing to do, but I suppose it's above and beyond the call of duty to sacrifice your personal time to help a complete stranger."

Now consider a scenario in which Poppy decides to help by delivering the popcorn kernel instead of the medicine:

> "Poppy, why don't you deliver that bottle of life-saving medicine?"
>
> "Eh, that's too much work."
>
> "What do you mean? It takes exactly as much work as delivering the popcorn kernel. Since you're doing the work anyway, why not provide the urgent, life-saving help instead of the trivial help?"
>
> "Huh, that's a good point."

(Side note: as philosophers since Plato have known, the beauty of writing dialogues is that you can script the replies to agree with you, thus making your own view appear more convincing.)

In the first scenario, the personal cost of helping serves as a moral excuse for not delivering the life-saving medicine.[3] We'd praise Poppy for taking the time out of her day to help; however, we might not blame her if she decides that she doesn't want to make the sacrifice. But in the second scenario Poppy has already accepted the personal cost of helping, so it cannot serve as a moral excuse for not delivering the medicine. Unless she has some special reason to deliver the popcorn kernel, Poppy would be wrong to deliver it instead of the medicine.

Think of it this way: other things being equal, why *wouldn't* you perform the action that does substantially more good? Insofar as we help, it's wrong to perform an act that is significantly and needlessly worse than an available alternative. By analogy, you might not be obligated to take the risk of diving into choppy waters to help some struggling swimmers. However, if you do take that risk and dive in, then you're obligated to help the four-year-old child to spare her from drowning rather than the Olympic swimmer to spare him from moderately sore muscles.[4]

If you're with me so far, consider next how your judgment lines up about another case:

> Vaughn elects to donate an hour of his day to making the world a better place. He has enough time to either (i) cast a vote, producing an expected social benefit of a few cents or (ii) work overtime and donate the proceeds to the Against Malaria Foundation, producing an expected four additional months of life for a child in Ghana.

The reason why Poppy would be wrong to deliver the popcorn instead of the medicine is also the reason why Vaughn would be wrong to vote instead of earning donatable income: it produces significantly and needlessly worse results.

Let's break this argument down. First, voting and comparable forms of political action typically produce significantly worse results than alternative uses of your time. Even uninformed voting—doing nothing more than registering, driving to the polls, waiting in line, voting, and driving home—might take you an hour. If you spent that hour earning somewhere near the average American wage, you'd make enough to donate the money needed to save about four months of life for a child dying of malaria.[5] So the expected value of your vote is significantly lower than the expected value of alternative uses of your time.

Maybe your job doesn't let you schedule any overtime, so you might be thinking that my argument doesn't apply to you. Even so, you have countless options that are far more beneficial than political activism. To earn more donatable income you could, for instance, occasionally drive your car for Uber and make around $15 per hour.[6] You could also assemble furniture for pay though TaskRabbit, do freelance proofreading and editing online through sites like Fiverr.com, develop skills to earn a raise, sort and sell your old stuff on eBay, cut coupons, renegotiate your cable bill, or prepare frozen meals for the week to shrink your restaurant expenses. If you prefer the direct route, you can volunteer at an understaffed shelter or kitchen. You can build homes with Habitat for Humanity. And this is all just off the top of my head. Think about your particular skills and situation and see what you can come up with. I'm confident that you'll unearth better uses of your time than politics.

Perhaps you're also concerned that the nonpolitical good you can do with the time it takes to cast a single vote is pretty small. The Against Malaria Foundation is a big charity after all, and one donation isn't likely to move the needle.

I have two replies. First, even doing something as small as earning enough money to give dozens of fresh socks to the homeless will tend to have a higher expected social benefit than political participation. Second, focus less on an individual act of political participation and more on the long-term *habit* of political participation. Consider what a lifetime of serious political engagement might include: regularly reading opinion pieces, watching news and debates, studying social science and political philosophy, taking steps to reduce one's partisan bias, attending rallies, discussing and linking to political articles on Facebook, going door-to-door for candidates, and so on. Now the opportunity costs of political engagement start piling up. You're spending lots of time and energy that you could reroute into truly effective altruism.

To make things more vivid, let's crunch some made-up numbers. Suppose you're 20 years old and decide to disengage from politics entirely. You use your spared time to earn extra money, working one hour of overtime per month at the average American wage of $22.50.[7] You invest that money wisely, earning an 8% return. By the time you're 60, you'll have accrued roughly $70,000. As things stand, the most efficient intervention to save a human life—again, supplying children with antimalarial mosquito nets—costs around $4,000.[8] Thus, by switching from politics to effective altruism, you could save 17 lives.

If you're still unmoved, ask yourself what you would do in the following scenario. One election night, as you're heading to the soon-to-be-closed polls on a deserted road, you spot a car that's crashed into a tree. The driver is bleeding profusely and needs to get to the hospital immediately or else he'll die. You can either vote in the presidential election or save the driver's life. What do you do?

I presume that you would save the driver instead of casting the vote. Now suppose, by some strange quirk of fate, that this same scenario plays itself out during each of the remaining presidential elections of your lifetime. Wouldn't you opt to save the life instead of casting the vote every single time?

Obviously I'm making a lot of assumptions here: I'm stipulating your wages, your return on investment, and the cost of saving a human life decades from now. So don't take my numbers too seriously. But this case illustrates a point that you *should* take seriously, namely that engaging in effective altruism does far more good than engaging in politics.

Political engagement, then, does significantly less good than alternative uses of your time. But is it *needlessly* worse than the alternatives? Think back to Poppy. If she made a promise to the food bank to deliver the popcorn, she might be obligated to honor the promise even though it does less good than delivering the medicine. More generally, if you have a special moral duty to perform the worse action, then you have at least some reason to perform it even though it leaves lots of good on the table. Or perhaps it would be extremely costly for Poppy to deliver the medicine instead of the popcorn—maybe the route is treacherous and poses risks to her safety.

However, most of us do not face these kinds of extenuating circumstances in the case of political abstention. I've argued in detail that you have no special moral duty to be politically engaged. For one, you can honor your obligation to contribute to the common good by performing actions that have nothing to do with politics. What's more, many of your compatriots are contributing to political *bads* rather than political goods, so their political participation doesn't generate any moral debts on your part anyway. And there's no symbolic duty to vote any more than there is a symbolic duty to wish upon a shooting star for world peace.

If effective altruism imposed significant personal costs, then you might be excused from effective altruism. However, I'm not asking you to allocate *more* time to effective altruism than what you're currently allocating to politics; instead, I'm merely asking you to reallocate your time away from politics and toward something more effective. To put the point differently, you need not change the *quantity* of help you're giving, only the *quality*.

Would a shift in the quality of your altruism hurt you? To the contrary: I'd say that it's costlier for you to engage in political altruism than effective altruism. As we've seen, political engagement is apt to make you more anxious, more hostile, and more intolerant. Evidence indicates that charitable giving, by contrast, makes you happier.[9]

On that note, let me leave you with a concluding thought.[10] Suppose you came across an abandoned well and heard a child's cry arise from within it. She tells you that she fell in a week ago and is close to death. You hustle back to your garage, grab some rope, lower it down into the well, and pull her out. There's no doubt that this experience is something you'd never forget. You'd feel happiness and pride whenever you reflect on that time that you saved the life of a child.

Most of you reading this book have it within your power to do likewise. You won't meet the child you spare from malaria, but she is spared just the same. Indeed, you have historically unprecedented opportunities to feed the hungry, heal the sick, enrich the poor, and literally save lives. You should seize them and leave politics behind.

Notes

INTRODUCTION

1. Pew Research Center 2007, 49.
2. Ibid.
3. Dalton 2008, 30.
4. Ingraham 2016.
5. New York Times Editorial Board 2018.
6. Reimer 2016.
7. Ibid.
8. See Gelman et al. 2012, 325 for the probability of a single vote in California being decisive in the presidential election.
9. See, e.g., Mill 1977; Rawls 1999, 206.
10. Pope Paul VI 1965.
11. U.S. Citizenship and Immigration Services 2019.
12. Ingraham 2016.
13. Schwitzgebel and Rust 2010.
14. See Hetherington 2008, 10.
15. As Jason Brennan (2012b, 5, fn 5) writes, "I sometimes worry that political philosophy suffers from parochialism, because it is written by political philosophers and thus reflects their peculiar concerns and interests. Plato suggested that philosophers should be kings, and Aristotle suggested that philosophizing was the highest form of life. They might be right, but we have to be suspicious, given that they are philosophers. Contemporary deliberative democrats often suggest that societies would be better if everyone acted like amateur political scientists and philosophers. They might be right, but we have to be suspicious when we hear this from political scientists and philosophers."

IN PURSUIT OF POLITICAL WISDOM

1. See Brennan (2016a, 163) and Huemer 2012 for other uses of the analogy between political participation and medical intervention.

2. Rasmussen Reports 2009.

3. Bartels 1996, 194.

4. Luskin 2002, 282.

5. See, e.g., Bennett 1988; Somin 2013, 33–36.

6. Somin 2013, 33.

7. Ibid.

8. Ibid., 19.

9. Ibid.

10. Ibid., 24.

11. Ibid., 32.

12. Ibid.

13. First Amendment Center of the Freedom Forum Institute 2018.

14. Bill of Rights Institute 2010.

15. DiJulio et al. 2015.

16. For a full account of American political ignorance (from which some of the previous information is drawn), see Somin 2013, chapter 1.

17. Petrosino et al. 2013.

18. Aos et al. 2004, 7.

19. MacAskill et al. 2015.

20. Ibid.

21. See Caplan 2007, chapter 2

22. Ibid., chapter 3.

23. See Caplan et al. 2013; Pew Research Center 2015, respectively.

24. Christandl and Fetchenhauer 2009, 384.

25. Ibid.

26. Romer 2008, 128.

27. I say more about the importance of economic growth and its role in alleviating poverty elsewhere. See Freiman 2017, chapter 4.

28. Anson 2018.

29. Rozenblit and Keil 2002.

30. Ibid., 521.

31. Fernbach et al. 2013.

32. Philosopher Adam Ferguson (1782, section 2) writes, "The forms of society are derived from an obscure and distant origin; they arise, long before the date of philosophy, from the instincts, not from the speculations of men. The crowd of mankind, are directed in their establishments and measures, by the circumstances in which they are placed; and seldom are turned from their way, to follow the plan of any single projector. Every step and every movement of the multitude, even in what are termed enlightened ages, are made with equal blindness to the future; and nations stumble upon establishments, which are indeed the result of human action, but not the execution of any human design."

33. See Dubner 2012.

34. Eskeland and Feyzioglu 1997.

35. The significance of this point is discussed in greater depth in Huemer 2012, 15.
36. Tetlock 2005.
37. Menand 2005.
38. Davis 2018.
39. Barnwell 2018.
40. Rozenblit and Keil 2002, 521.
41. Huemer 2012, 12.
42. On shortcuts, see for instance Lupia and McCubbins 1998; Christiano 2015, 257–260.
43. Popkin 1991, 3.
44. Achen and Bartels 2016, 39.
45. Hooks 2018.
46. Ibid.
47. Ibid.
48. For instance, it may be the case that some people are "superforecasters" who can make predictions that are much better than pure chance. See Tetlock and Gardner 2015. So perhaps the problem of getting accurate forecasts is not insurmountable; however, it will require researching forecasters rather than, say, trusting the pundits on television.
49. For evidence that our partisan commitments affect our judgments of expertise, see Kahan et al. 2011.
50. Somin (2015, 386) writes, "Unfortunately, the opinion leaders voters turn to are rarely ones with deep expertise on public policy or a strong track record of accurate predictions. Rather, they tend to be those that are most entertaining and most likely to reinforce the voters' preexisting views—people like Rush Limbaugh on the right or Jon Stewart on the left, among others (Somin 2013, 99–100). . . . It is extremely rare for voters to search out opinion leaders with political perspectives significantly divergent from the voters' own."
51. On differences in preferences, see Delli Carpini and Keeter 1996, chapter 6; Althaus 1998; on the effects of political education on political opinions see Sturgis 2003; on voting behavior, see Bartels 1996.
52. As Somin (2013, 99) writes, "Since the whole point of relying on opinion leaders is to economize on information costs, the voter is unlikely to invest heavily in researching the leaders' qualifications."
53. See PhilPapers.org, "Abortion."

WE'RE ALL PARTISAN HACKS

1. For a sampling of the evidence for pervasive politically motivated reasoning, see Lord et al. 1979; Bartels 2002; Redlawsk 2002; Cohen 2003; Taber and Lodge 2006; Sherman and Cohen 2006; Gerber and Huber

2010; Nyhan and Reifler 2010; Greene 2013; Kahan et al. 2010; Kahan et al. 2011; Kahan et al. 2013; Kahan 2013; Kahan 2016a; Westfall et al. 2015; Achen and Bartels 2016; Van Bavel and Pereira 2018.

2. Somin 2013; Mason 2015; Brennan 2016a.

3. Hastorf and Cantril 1954 (reported in Kahan et al. 2012).

4. Kahan et al. 2012.

5. Ibid., 880.

6. Ibid.

7. Ibid., 883.

8. Ibid.

9. Although politically motivated reasoning looks similar to confirmation bias, they are importantly different. Dan Kahan explains: "Someone who engages in politically motivated reasoning will predictably form beliefs consistent with the position that fits her predispositions. Because she will also selectively credit new information based on its congeniality to that same position, it will look like she is deriving the likelihood ratio from her priors. However, the correlation is spurious: a 'third variable'—her motivation to form beliefs congenial to her identity—is the 'cause' of both her priors and her likelihood ratio assessment." Kahan 2016a, 5. Emphasis in the original.

10. Taber and Lodge 2006. Also, the more politically knowledgeable you are, the less likely you are to be exposed to contrary political viewpoints. See Mutz 2006, 32.

11. Kaplan et al. 2016.

12. Ibid., 5.

13. Ibid., 8.

14. Quoted in McRaney 2017.

15. Frimer et al. 2017.

16. Lord et al. 1979. See also Taber and Lodge 2006.

17. Gampa et al. 2019.

18. Westen et al. 2006, 1956.

19. Achen and Bartels 2016, 18.

20. Cohen 2003.

21. Ibid., 811.

22. Ibid. For similar findings, see Verkuyten and Maliepaard 2013; Munro et al. 2013.

23. Pew Research Center 2017.

24. Ibid.

25. Newport 2009.

26. Ibid.

27. Freeder et al. 2019, 288.

28. For an extended discussion of this issue and its philosophical implications, see Joshi 2019. See also Brennan 2016a, 41; Huemer 2016.

29. Joshi 2019, 25.

30. Kahan 2016a.

31. Ibid., 2. Emphasis in the original.
32. Ibid. Kahan cites Sherman and Cohen 2006.
33. As Jonathan Haidt puts it, "To the extent policy beliefs become markers of group membership, we can guarantee that every group is wrong on many points but will never know it." Quoted in Doherty 2018.
34. Bertrand Russell (2009, 140) writes, "It is very easy to give examples of true beliefs that are not knowledge. There is the man who looks at a clock which is not going, though he thinks it is, and who happens to look at it at the moment when it is right; this man acquires a true belief as to the time of day, but cannot be said to have knowledge. There is the man who believes, truly, that the last name of the Prime Minister in 1906 began with a B, but who believes this because he thinks that Balfour was Prime Minister then, whereas in fact it was Campbell-Bannerman. There is the lucky optimist who, having bought a ticket for a lottery, has an unshakeable conviction that he will win, and, being lucky, does win. Such instances can be multiplied indefinitely, and show that you cannot claim to have known merely because you turned out to be right."
35. Huemer 2012, 25. Emphasis in the original.
36. For a criticism of effective altruism, see Deaton 2015. For a defense of effective altruism against various objections, see Karnofsky 2015.
37. Pronin, Lin, and Ross 2002.
38. Ibid.
39. Ibid.
40. West et al. 2012.
41. Perkins et al. 1991.
42. Ibid., 95.
43. Kahan et al. 2017.
44. At one point, there was some controversy about whether the motivated numeracy study would replicate. See Kahan and Peters 2017 for a reply to these concerns.
45. Kahan 2013.
46. Gampa et al. 2019.
47. Kahan 2015, 12.
48. Bolsen et al. 2015; Drummond and Fischhoff 2017.
49. Kahan 2013.
50. Braman et al. 2012; Kahan 2013; Nisbet et al. 2015.
51. Kahan 2013.
52. For an overview, see Flynn, Nyhan, and Reifler, 2017.
53. Lodge and Taber 2000; Redlawsk 2002; Nyhan and Reifler 2010; Bail et al. 2018.
54. See, e.g., Schkade et al. 2007; Mutz 2006, chapter 4. For a philosophical critique of deliberative democracy, see Pincione and Tesón 2006.
55. Bullock et al. 2015; Prior et al. 2015. On the limitations of these studies, see Kahan 2016b, 6–8.

56. See Sparks et al. 2010; Nyhan and Reifler 2019.
57. See Coleman 2011, chapters 3 and 4.
58. Fernbach et al. 2013.

THE COSTS AND BENEFITS OF POLITICAL PARTICIPATION

1. On effective altruism, see, e.g., Singer 2015; MacAskill 2015.
2. See Gelman et al. 2012. Older estimates, which use a different formula for calculating decisiveness, give far lower odds. See, e.g., Downs 1957; Riker and Ordeshook 1968; Ferejohn and Fiorina 1974; Meehl 1977; Owen and Grofman 1984; Aldrich 1993; Brennan and Lomasky 1993, 56–57; Green and Shapiro 1994; Carling 1995; Gelman et al. 1998; Shachar and Nalebuff 1999; Mueller 2003, 305; Brennan 2012c, 17–28.
3. Dubner and Levitt 2005. See also Mulligan and Hunter 2003, 48–50.
4. See, e.g., Gonzales 2013; Collins 2016.
5. Mulligan and Hunter 2003.
6. Julia Maskivker (2018, 414), for example, defends voting partly by an appeal to an argument that "our actions matter even when they are not individually powerful to determine an outcome by themselves." See also Beerbohm 2012, chapter 2; Estlund 2008, 272.
7. See Guglielmi et al. 2018.
8. Research from political scientist Erica Chenoweth suggests that it only takes about 3.5% of the population to actively participate in (nonviolent) protests to ensure large-scale political change (see the discussion in Robson 2019). Note, however, that this means that it would take roughly 11 million active protestors to bring about nationwide political change in the United States—i.e., about ten times the number of protestors in the March for Science.
9. For further discussion of this idea, see Gutting 2016.
10. See, e.g., Lomasky and Brennan 2000, 65–67; Brennan 2012c, 19–20.
11. Lomasky and Brennan (2000, 66) stress the relevance of the opportunity cost of voting when considering whether it is an effective way of serving one's interests.
12. On this point, see ibid., 67.
13. Parfit 1984, 74–75.
14. Barry 1978, 39. Emphasis in the original.
15. See, e.g., MacAskill 2015, 87.
16. On the lottery analogy, see Brennan 2016c.
17. For an argument along these lines, see Guerrero 2010.
18. Dahl 1990; Noel 2010.
19. Noyes 2018.

20. For discussion of this point, see Brennan 2012c, 53.
21. Economist Mancur Olson (1971, 64) explains: "Even if the member of a large group were to neglect his own interests entirely, he still would not rationally contribute toward the provision of any collective or public good, since his own contribution would not be perceptible. . . . He would know that this sacrifice would not bring a noticeable benefit to anyone. Such a rational [actor], however unselfish, would not make such a futile and pointless sacrifice, but he would allocate his philanthropy in order to have a perceptible effect on someone."
22. See, e.g., Singer 2015; MacAskill 2015.
23. See *Givewell.org*, "Top Charities"
24. See MacAskill 2015, 220, fn 51.
25. See *Trading Economics*, "United States Average Hourly Wages," 2018.
26. Even if I *do* have substantial influence on the moral behavior of others, I should still probably abstain from political activism and focus on philanthropic engagement. Persuading a dozen people to vote still isn't going to move the needle in an election. But persuading them to donate some of their income to the Against Malaria Foundation would literally save lives.
27. Maskivker 2018, 418.
28. On the duty of easy aid, see ibid., 411.
29. Ibid., 413.
30. Ibid., 418.
31. Ibid.
32. Maskivker 2018, 414.
33. Ibid., 417.
34. Alkire et al. 2018.
35. Gomberg 2002, 64.
36. Srinivasan 2015.
37. Ibid., 97. McMahan (ibid.) writes that we wouldn't blame "a doctor who treats the victims of a war for failing to devote his efforts instead to eliminating the root causes of war."
38. Peter Singer (2009, 36) writes, "If, after investigating the causes of global poverty and considering what approach is most likely to reduce it, you really believe that a more revolutionary change is needed, then it would make sense to put your time, energy, and money into organizations promoting that revolution in the global economic system. But this is a practical question, and if there is little chance of achieving the kind of revolution you are seeking, then you need to look around for a strategy with better prospects of actually helping some poor people."
39. Cohen 2000, 19.
40. For further discussion of this point, see MacAskill 2015, 89–94.
41. See MacAskill 2015, 86. See also Edlin et al. 2007; Edlin et al. 2008.
42. MacAskill 2015, 87.
43. Ibid., 86.
44. Ibid.

45. See, e.g., Brennan and Lomasky 2006, 233.
46. MacAskill 2015, 86.
47. Ibid.
48. Brennan and Lomasky 2000, 71.
49. Ibid.
50. Ibid.
51. For discussion of these sorts of problems, see ibid., 69–72.
52. See *Politifact* 2019 if you'd like to review the records of recent presidents.
53. Kahan et al. 2017.
54. Fernbach et al. 2013.
55. MacAskill et al. 2015.
56. See, e.g., Lord et al. 1979.
57. Kahan et al. 2011; Somin 2013, 99–100.
58. Huemer 2012, 23. Emphasis in the original.
59. Even if the election of your favored candidate benefits Americans on average, it will also harm particular Americans who would not have been harmed had the candidate not been elected. For instance, a given policy might save more lives than the alternative while still resulting in the death of particular people who would not have died under the alternative policy. Although I will not pursue this point here, it does raise further difficulties for advocates of political participation.
60. Lomasky and Brennan (2000, 72) also note this point about arguments that attempt to ground a duty to vote in the consequences of casting a vote.

FAIRNESS AND FREE RIDING

1. See Wagoner 2016.
2. For information about Kaepernick's donations, see ibid.
3. 2000, 75ff.
4. For an interesting discussion of generalization reasoning and Kantian ethics, see Feldman 2003. Rule consequentialists also endorse a view that employs something like generalization reasoning—right actions are those that conform to the rules whose widespread acceptance would lead to the best consequences. So you shouldn't lie even in a particular case where lying has good consequences because a prohibition on lying is one of the rules that would produce the best consequences when widely accepted.
5. See, e.g., Lomasky and Brennan 2000, 76.
6. As Lomasky and Brennan (2000, 77) put it, "Strictly speaking, what makes an ungeneralizable action wrong is not that it fails the generalization test. Rather, it fails the generalization test because of underlying unfairness, and it is the unfairness that accounts for the action's wrongness."

7. For more detailed treatments of this principle see, e.g., Hart 1955; Rawls 1964; Klosko 1992. For a fairness argument specifically in support of political participation see Waldron 1998, 318.

8. Estlund 2008, 272.

9. Lomasky and Brennan 2000, 78.

10. Ibid., 76.

11. This point should assuage whatever lingering worries you have about your abstention setting a bad example for others. Even if your abstention does somehow encourage others to abstain, you'll raise the value of the vote and incentivize an offsetting increase in participation.

12. Brennan 2012c, 39.

13. Moreover, as Jason Brennan argues, if you are likely to make a high-quality political contribution because you are particularly informed or unbiased, then your abstention will make overall democratic participation marginally worse. Brennan 2012c, 39.

14. Schmidtz 2006, 93

15. Brennan and Lomasky 2006, 231.

16. Brennan 2012c, 53.

17. Zhu 2015.

18. Ibid., 295.

19. Ibid.

20. McMahan 2016, 97.

21. Brennan and Lomasky (2006, 231) write, "Perhaps only a modest proportion of the populace needs to be engaged in political activity to promote the general welfare. More strongly, the general welfare may be better promoted by prevailing low levels of activity than it would be with either considerably less or considerably greater participation. If this hypothesis is correct, politics will resemble numerous other activities to which people lend their attention. Here is another batch of hypotheses: the number of people who grow crops, practice dentistry, perform in choral societies, or study the philosophical foundations of republicanism is roughly optimal; that is, deviations in either direction by more than an order of magnitude would have deleterious results."

22. Maskivker 2016.

23. Smith 2003, 1.2.2.

24. On this point see Brennan 2012c, 59.

25. For a detailed discussion, see Brown 2018.

26. Maskivker 2016.

27. Brown 2018, 4.

28. Ibid., 8. Emphasis in the original.

29. Ibid.

30. Ibid.

31. As a side note, one worry about Brown's account of reciprocity is that a citizen who dedicates herself to single issue political advocacy (e.g., the

humane treatment of refugees) would be regarded as making an inadequate contribution because she fails to satisfy the scope condition.

32. Becker 2014, 106.
33. Ibid., 110.
34. Ibid., 111.
35. Brennan and Hill 2014, 81.
36. As Garret Cullity (2008, 13) puts the point, "[I]f a good is not being produced and supplied as it ought, that undermines the case for thinking that refusing to pay for it is unfair."
37. See *FairVote* 2019.
38. See Hetherington 2008, 10.
39. Bartels 1996, 194.
40. Pew Research Center 2017.
41. Somin 2013, 80.
42. See, e.g., Plumer 2019.
43. Philips 2015.
44. Stern 2018.
45. Caplan 2007, 157.
46. Rasmussen Reports 2009,
47. Kahan et al. 2011.
48. I'll also note that addressing climate change is toward the bottom of the list of priorities for both Democrats and Republicans (although it is ranked as a lower priority for Republicans). See Newport 2016.
49. On the gap between public and scientific opinion on nuclear energy, see Pew Research Center 2015.
50. Kahan et al. 2011.
51. Caplan 2007, 139.
52. For a related discussion, see Huemer 2012, 19.
53. Kahan 2016a, 2. Emphasis in the original.
54. Elsewhere Kahan (2016b, 7) writes, "The only material stake most ordinary people have in the content of their beliefs about policy-relevant facts is the contribution they make to the experience of *being* a particular sort of person. The *beliefs* a person forms about the deterrent effect of concealed-carry laws on violent crime, the contribution of human activity to global warming, and like 'facts' reliably dispose her to *act* in ways that signify her identity-defining group commitments to those who will judge her character accordingly. Failing to attend to information in a manner that generates such beliefs can severely compromise someone's well-being—not because the beliefs she will form in that case will be factually *wrong*, but because they will convey the wrong *message* about who she is and whose side she is on." Emphasis in the original.
55. For an argument along these lines, see Brennan 2009.
56. Achen and Bartels 2016, 4.
57. Iyengar and Krupenkin 2018, 211.
58. Ibid., 215.

59. On evidence for anger as a motivation for political engagement, see Valentino et al. 2011.
60. For a defense of such a duty, see Singer 1972.

POLITICAL ABSTENTION AND COMPLICITY IN INJUSTICE

1. Beerbohm 2012, 75.
2. Ibid., 72.
3. For the sake of argument, I'll set aside my worries about the accuracy of our political beliefs. It's safe to say that our government produces many unjust policies even if it is hard to know which specific ones are unjust.
4. Beerbohm 2012, 64.
5. Ibid.
6. Beerbohm (2012, 73) writes, "Our nonresistance itself is a kind of sponsorship, however small." See also Maskivker 2018, 414; Shklar 1990.
7. Maskivker 2018, 416.
8. Ibid., 417.
9. Beerbohm 2012, 73.
10. Ibid., 72.
11. Ibid.
12. Ibid.
13. A related idea, which I will not explore, asserts that political abstention is itself a form of resistance to political injustice. See, e.g., Hanna 2009; Brennan and Lomasky 2000, 83–84; Goldman 1999, 215.
14. Estés 2003.
15. Tea 2017.
16. 2012, 75.

THE MORALITY OF THE MESSAGE

1. Quoted in Brennan 2012a.
2. Benn 1978, 19. For criticism, see Barry 1978, 47. See also Waldron 1998, 317.
3. Easterbrook 1997.
4. Lomasky and Brennan 2000, 82. Emphasis in the original.
5. Ibid., 83.
6. Benn considers the objection that one need not participate in politics formally to express the relevant attitudes. He replies, "To be understood as political a participatory act must either be calculated to effect a political outcome, such as a change of policy, or it must be more or less ritualistic, an act conventionally understood to betoken a concern

for some principle or ideal characteristically and importantly at issue in governmental decision-making." Benn 1978, 20. However, I would argue that today bumper stickers and tweets *are* conventionally understood as conveying one's allegiance to a political principle.

7. Brian Barry (1978, 47) objects that justifying political participation in terms of expression "is a charter for frivolity. It offers aid and comfort to the politics of the beautiful people—the radical chic of the Boston-Washington corridor and the London-Oxbridge triangle. The last fifteen years have seen too much of people for whom politics is a sort of psychic adventure playground, and in my view political philosophers should be trying to knock the props out from under the self-esteem of these folk rather than rationalising it. As between Lady Bountiful and Leonard Bernstein give me Lady Bountiful—at least the poor got some soup and blankets out of her."

8. Joint United Nations Programme on HIV/AIDS 2010, 143.

9. Thanks to Ryan Davis for suggesting this sort of case.

10. 2000, 82.

11. Schmidtz is quoted in Brennan 2012a, 148.

12. Holmes 2017.

13. Ibid.

14. I owe this example to Philip Swenson.

15. Galanes 2015.

16. Marotta 2018.

17. See, e.g., Hursthouse 1999; Annas 2011; Badhwar 2014, especially chapters 6 and 7.

18. Hursthouse 1999, 196; Foot 2003; Annas 2005.

19. See Hursthouse 1999, part III.

20. Ibid., 209.

21. Ibid., 210. Emphasis in the original.

22. I'll note that there are powerful criticisms of this conception of virtue but I won't pursue them here. See, for instance, Copp and Sobel 2004; Millgram 2005.

23. Hursthouse 1999, 209.

24. Ibid., 210. Emphasis removed.

25. Hursthouse 1999; Annas 2005.

26. For a similar point, see Brennan 2016b, 250–251.

27. Badhwar 2014, 159.

28. Foot 2002, 5.

29. See Lomasky and Brennan 2000, 82 for an interpretation along these lines.

POLITICAL IGNORANCE IS BLISS

1. Rawls 1999, 206.

2. Soroka and McAdams 2015.

3. Winerman 2017.

4. Pinto et al. 2019, 28.

5. Ibid.

6. Smith et al. 2019, 11.

7. Long and Sedley 1987, 62a.

8. Mason 2018, 14. Emphasis in the original.

9. Iyengar and Westwood 2015, 705.

10. Mason 2018, 14.

11. Mason 2016.

12. Groenendyk 2018, 170.

13. Groenendyk 2012.

14. Moreover, hostility toward the out party is an increasingly powerful motivation for political engagement: "Today it is outgroup animus rather than ingroup favoritism that drives political behavior" (Iyengar and Krupenkin 2018, 211).

15. Mill 1977, chapter 8.

16. Brennan 2016a, 232.

17. Cox and Jones 2016.

18. Reuters 2017.

19. CNN 2017.

20. Pew Research Center 2014a.

21. Malhotra and Huber 2017.

22. Kleinfeld et al. 2018.

23. Iyengar et al. 2012, 418.

24. On "affective polarization," see, e.g., Iyengar et al. 2012; Iyengar and Westwood 2015; Mason 2015.

25. Hart 2018.

26. Kalmoe and Mason 2019, 17–18.

27. Ibid., 17, 22.

28. For further discussion of this point, see Freiman 2017, chapter 8.

29. Iyengar and Westwood 2015.

30. Gift and Gift 2015.

31. Iyengar and Westwood 2015.

32. McConnell et al. 2018.

33. Iyengar et al. 2019, 134.

34. Martherus et al. 2019.

35. Ibid.

36. Kalmoe and Mason 2019, 17–18.

37. See Kteily et al. 2015; Bandura et al. 1975; Kelman 1973, respectively.

38. Kalmoe and Mason 2019, 17, 23.

39. Thanks to Jason Brennan for encouraging me to make this argument explicit.

40. Ibid., 17–18.

41. Ahler and Sood 2018.

42. Ibid., 968.

43. Ibid.
44. Levendusky and Malhotra 2016.
45. Groenendyk 2012.
46. See Epley and Dunning 2000; Pronin, Lin, and Ross 2002, respectively.
47. Pronin, Puccio, and Ross 2002, 665.
48. Quoted in Doherty 2018.
49. Huddy et al. 2007.
50. MacKuen et al. 2010; Weeks 2015, respectively.
51. Along these lines, Jason Brennan (2016a, 129) suggests that we can imagine a world where "instead of viewing the president as majestic or the office of the presidency as deserving reverence, people merely think of the president as the chief public goods administrator."
52. Pew Research Center 2014b.
53. Van Bavel and Pereira 2018, 219
54. For information about effective altruism groups, you can visit https://app.effectivealtruism.org/groups/resources/resources-and-support

CONCLUSION

1. There are other arguments for the wrongness of political participation that I will not explore here. Perhaps abstention is justified as a form of protest against an unjust system. Or maybe it is wrong to participate when you have reason to think that your political aims are biased or ill-informed. On this latter argument see Brennan 2009.

2. For discussion, see Kagan 1989, 16; Pummer 2016; Horton 2017; Sinclair 2018.

3. On this idea, see Pummer 2016. I should say that I'm not convinced that the small personal cost does, in fact, excuse Poppy from providing the large benefit to the child. However, let's assume that it does for the sake of argument.

4. Thomas Sinclair (2018) argues that our judgments about these sorts of cases do not support a conditional obligation of effective altruism, whereby we have a duty to allocate our help to causes that maximize social benefits. Instead, we have a duty to rescue, a duty from which you can be excused if the personal costs of honoring it are excessive. However, if you accept these personal costs, then you are not granted moral release from the duty to rescue. Thus, Sinclair can conclude that it is wrong to not save the drowning child in the case above without appealing to anything like a conditional obligation of effective altruism. I take no stand on whether Sinclair's analysis is correct; however, I will say that even if it is, my case against political participation stands. The reason, in brief, is because we have a duty to make moderate personal sacrifices to prevent others from experiencing severe harm. Thus, by voting instead

of earning donatable income, Vaughn would be neglecting his duty—a neglect that could *not* be justified by an appeal to personal cost given that he has already accepted an equivalent personal cost. For a defense of the duty to prevent severe harm, see Singer 1972.

5. A rough estimate of the lowest cost required to save a "quality adjusted life year" is $68.90. See MacAskill 2015, 220. The average American hourly wage in 2018 was about $22.50. See *Trading Economics*, "United States Average Hourly Wages," 2018.

6. *Ridester's 2018 Independent Driver Earnings Survey*, 2018.

7. See *Trading Economics*, "United States Average Hourly Wages," 2018.

8. GiveWell Cost-Effectiveness Analysis—Version 4, 2019.

9. See, e.g., Dunn et al. 2008; Aknin et al. 2010.

10. This case is inspired by a similar one in MacAskill 2015, 53.

Achen, Christopher and Larry Bartels, *Democracy for Realists: Why Elections do not Produce Responsive Government.* Princeton: Princeton University Press, 2016.

Ahler, Douglas and Gaurav Sood, "The Parties in Our Heads: Misperceptions About Party Composition and Their Consequences," *The Journal of Politics* 80 (2018): 964–981.

Aknin, Lara, Christopher Barrington-Leigh, Elizabeth Dunn, John Helliwell, Robert Biswas-Diener, Imelda Kemeza, Paul Nyende, Claire Ashton-James, and Michael I. Norton, "Prosocial Spending and Well-Being: Cross-Cultural Evidence for a Psychological Universal," *Harvard Business School Working Paper* 11–038 (2010).

Aldrich, John, "Rational Choice and Turnout," *American Journal of Political Science* 37 (1993): 246–278.

Alkire, Sabina, Florent Bédécarrats, Angus Deaton, Gaël Giraud, Isabelle Guérin, Barbara Harriss-White, James Heckman, Jason Hickel, Naila Kabeer, Solène Morvant-Roux, Judea Pearl, Cécile Renouard, François Roubaud, Jean-Michel Servet, and Joseph Stiglitz, "Buzzwords and Tortuous Impact Studies Won't Fix a Broken Aid System," *The Guardian* 7.26.18. Accessed 5.30.19. Available online at: www.theguardian.com/global-development/2018/jul/16/buzzwords-crazes-broken-aid-system-poverty

Althaus, Scott, "Information Effects in Collective Preferences," *American Political Science Review* 92 (1998): 545–558.

Annas, Julia, "Virtue Ethics: What Kind of Naturalism?" in Stephen Gardiner, ed. *Virtue Ethics, Old and New.* Ithaca, NY: Cornell University Press, 2005, 11–29.

Annas, Julia, *Intelligent Virtue.* Oxford: Oxford University Press, 2011.

Anson, Ian, "Partisanship, Political Knowledge, and the Dunning-Kruger Effect," *Political Psychology* 39 (2018): 1173–1192.

Aos, Steve, Roxanne Lieb, Jim Mayfield, Marna Miller, and Annie Pennucci, *Benefits and Costs of Prevention and Early Intervention Programs for Youth.* Olympia: Washington State Institute for Public Policy, 2004.

Badhwar, Neera, *Well-Being: Happiness in a Worthwhile Life*. Oxford: Oxford University Press, 2014.

Bail, Christopher, Lisa Argyle, Taylor Brown, John Bumpus, Haohan Chen, M.B. Fallin Hunzaker, Jaemin Lee, Marcus Mann, Friedolin Merhout, and Alexander Volfovsky, "Exposure to Opposing Views on Social Media Can Increase Political Polarization," *Proceedings of the National Academy of Sciences* 115 (2018): 9216–9221.

Bandura, Albert, Bill Underwood, and Michael Fromson, "Disinhibition of Aggression Through Diffusion of Responsibility and Dehumanization of Victims," *Journal of Research in Personality* 9 (1975): 253–269.

Barry, Brian, "Comment," in Stanley Benn, ed. *Political Participation: A Discussion of Political Rationality*. Canberra: Australian National University Press, 1978, 37–48.

Bartels, Larry, "Uninformed Votes: Information Effects in Presidential Elections," *American Journal of Political Science* 40 (1996): 194–230.

Bartels, Larry, "Beyond the Running Tally: Partisan Bias in Political Perceptions," *Political Behavior* 24 (2002): 117–150.

Becker, Lawrence, *Reciprocity*. New York: Routledge, 2014, 106.

Beerbohm, Eric, *In Our Name: The Ethics of Democracy*. Princeton: Princeton University Press, 2012.

Benn, Stanley "The Problematic Rationality of Political Participation," in Stanley Benn, ed. *Political Participation: A Discussion of Political Rationality*. Canberra: Australian National University Press, 1978, 1–22.

Bennett, Stephen, "'Know-Nothings' Revisited: The Meaning of Political Ignorance Today," *Social Science Quarterly* 69 (1988): 476–492.

Bill Barnwell, "History Tells Us the NFL is Terrible at Evaluating Quarterbacks. Here's What It Means for 2018," ESPN 4.10.18. Accessed 7.3.19. Available online at: www.espn.com/nfl/story/_/id/23039883/history-tells-us-nfl-terrible-evaluating-quarterbacks-means-2018-draft-prospects#Part1

Bill of Rights Institute, "42 Percent of Americans Attribute Communist Slogan to America's Founding Documents," 12.15.10. Accessed 5.27.19. Available online at: http://billofrightsinstitute.org/wp-content/uploads/2011/12/42-Percent-of-Americans-Attribute-Communist-Slogan-to-Americas-Founding-Documents.pdf

Bolsen, Toby, James Druckman, and Fay Lomax Cook, "Citizens, 'Scientists', and Policy Advisors' Beliefs about Global Warming," *The ANNALS of the American Academy of Political and Social Science* 658 (2015): 271–295.

Braman, Donald, Dan Kahan, Ellen Peters, Maggie Wittlin, Paul Slovic, Lisa Larrimore Ouellette, and Gregory Mandel, "The Polarizing Impact of Science Literacy and Numeracy on Perceived Climate Change Risks," *Nature Climate Change* 2 (2012): 732–735.

Brennan, Geoffrey, "Climate Change: A Rational Choice Politics View," *The Australian Journal of Agricultural and Resource Economics* 53 (2009): 309–326.

Brennan, Geoffrey and Loren Lomasky, *Democracy and Decision*. Cambridge: Cambridge University Press, 1993.

Brennan, Geoffrey and Loren Lomasky, "Against Reviving Republicanism," *Politics, Philosophy, and Economics* 5 (2006): 221–252.

Brennan, Jason, "Polluting the Polls: When Citizens Should Not Vote," *Australasian Journal of Philosophy* 87 (2009): 535–549.

Brennan, Jason, *Libertarianism: What Everyone Needs to Know*. New York: Oxford University Press, 2012a.

Brennan, Jason, "Political Liberty: Who Needs It," *Social Philosophy and Policy* 29 (2012b): 1–27.

Brennan, Jason, *The Ethics of Voting*. Princeton: Princeton University Press, 2012c.

Brennan, Jason, *Against Democracy*. Princeton: Princeton University Press, 2016a.

Brennan, Jason, "Do Markets Corrupt?" in Jennifer Baker and Mark White, eds. *Economics and the Virtues: Building a New Moral Foundation*. Oxford: Oxford University Press, 2016b, 236–255.

Brennan, Jason, "The Ethics and Rationality of Voting," in Edward N. Zalta, ed. *Stanford Encyclopedia of Philosophy*, 2016c. Accessed 12.11.19. Available online at: https://plato.stanford.edu/entries/voting/

Brennan, Jason and Lisa Hill, *Compulsory Voting: For and Against*. Cambridge: Cambridge University Press, 2014.

Brown, Brookes, "Beyond Profit and Politics: Reciprocity and the Role of For-Profit Business," *Journal of Business Ethics* (2018): 1–13. Available online at: https://doi.org/10.1007/s10551-018-3777-6

Bullock, John, Alan Gerber, Seth Hill, and Gregory Huber, "Partisan Bias in Factual Beliefs About Politics," *Quarterly Journal of Political Science* 10 (2015): 519–578.

Caplan, Bryan, *The Myth of the Rational Voter*. Princeton: Princeton University Press, 2007.

Caplan, Bryan, Eric Crampton, Wayne Grove, and Ilya Somin, "Systematically Biased Beliefs about Political Influence: Evidence from the Perceptions of Political Influence on Policy Outcomes Survey," *PS: Political Science & Politics* 46 (2013): 760–767.

Carling, Alan, "The Paradox of Voting and the Theory of Social Evolution," in Keith Dowding and Desmond King, eds. *Preferences, Institutions and Rational Choice*. Oxford: Clarendon Press, 1995, 20–43.

Christandl, Fabian and Detlef Fetchenhauer, "How Laypeople and Experts Misperceive the Effect of Economic Growth," *Journal of Economic Psychology* 30 (2009): 381–392.

Christiano, Thomas, "Voter Ignorance is not Necessarily a Problem," *Critical Review* 27 (2015): 253–269.

CNN, "March 1–4, 2017 Poll," 3.9.17. Accessed 6.17.19. Available online at: http://i2.cdn.turner.com/cnn/2017/images/03/09/rel4e.-.politics.pdf

Cohen, G.A. "If You're An Egalitarian, How Come You're So Rich?" *The Journal of Ethics* 4 (2000): 1–26.

Cohen, Geoffrey, "Party Over Policy: The Dominating Impact of Group Influence on Political Beliefs," *Journal of Personality and Social Psychology* 85 (2003): 808–822.

Coleman, Peter, *The Five Percent: Finding Solutions to Seemingly Impossible Conflicts*. New York: PublicAffairs, 2011.

Collins, Michael, "Fewer and Fewer U.S. House Seats Have Any Competition," *USA Today* 11.4.16. Accessed 5.30.19. Available online at: www.usatoday.com/story/news/politics/elections/2016/11/04/fewer-and-fewer-us-house-seats-have-any-competition/93295358/

Copp, David and David Sobel, "Morality and Virtue: An Assessment of Some Recent Work in Virtue Ethics," *Ethics* 114 (2004): 514–554.

Cox, Daniel and Robert Jones, "'Merry Christmas' vs. 'Happy Holidays': Republicans and Democrats are Polar Opposites," *PRRI* 12.19.16. Accessed 6.17.19. Available online at: www.prri.org/research/poll-post-election-holiday-war-christmas/

Cullity, Garrett, "Public Goods and Fairness," *Australasian Journal of Philosophy* 86, no. 1 (2008): 1–21.

Dahl, Robert, "The Myth of the Presidential Mandate," *Political Science Quarterly* 105 (1990): 355–372.

Dalton, Russell, *The Good Citizen: How a Younger Generation is Reshaping American Politics*. Thousand Oaks, CA: CQ Press, 2008.

Davis, Scott, "Dallas Cowboys Coach Says he Won't Draft Offensive Linemen if They Don't Know the Clever Way to Get Ketchup Out of a Bottle," *Business Insider* 5.20.18. Accessed 7.3.19. Available online at: www.businessinsider.com/dallas-cowboys-paul-alexander-offensive-lineman-ketchup-2018-5

Deaton, Angus, "The Logic of Effective Altruism," *Boston Review* 7.1.15. Accessed 5.30.19. Available online at: http://bostonreview.net/forum/logic-effective-altruism/angus-deaton-response-effective-altruism

Delli Carpini, Michael and Scott Keeter, *What Americans Know About Politics and Why it Matters*. New Haven: Yale University Press, 1996.

DiJulio, Bianca, Jamie Firth, and Mollyann Brodie, "Data Note: Americans' Views On the U.S. Role in Global Health," *Henry J Kaiser Family Foundation* 1.23.15. Accessed 6.7.19. Available online at: www.kff.org/global-health-policy/poll-finding/data-note-americans-views-on-the-u-s-role-in-global-health/

Doherty, Brian, "Jonathan Haidt Wants His Students to Love Dissent—and John Stuart Mill," *Reason Magazine* August/September 2018. Accessed 6.17.19. Available online at: https://reason.com/2018/08/01/jonathan-haidt-wants-his-stude

Downs, Anthony, *An Economic Theory of Democracy*. New York: Harper and Row, 1957.

Drummond, Caitlin and Baruch Fischhoff, "Individuals With Greater Science Literacy and Education Have More Polarized Beliefs on Controversial Science Topics," *Proceedings of the National Academy of Sciences* 114 (2017): 9587–9592.

Dubner, Stephen, "The Cobra Effect," *Freakonomics.com* 10.11.12. Accessed 6.7.19. Available online at: http://freakonomics.com/podcast/the-cobra-effect-a-new-freakonomics-radio-podcast/

Dubner, Stephen and Steven Levitt, "Why Vote?" *The New York Times* 11.6.05. Accessed 6.4.19. Available online at: www.nytimes.com/2005/11/06/magazine/why-vote.html?smid=nytcore-ios-share

Dunn, Elizabeth, Lara Aknin, and Michael Norton, "Spending Money on Others Promotes Happiness," *Science* 319 (2008): 1687–1688.

Easterbrook, Gregg, "Forgotten Benefactor of Humanity," *The Atlantic* January 1997. Accessed 1.5.19. Available online at: www.theatlantic.com/magazine/archive/1997/01/forgotten-benefactor-of-humanity/306101/

Edlin, Aaron, Andrew Gelman, and Noah Kaplan, "Voting as a Rational Choice: Why and How People Vote to Improve the Well-Being of Others," *Rationality and Society* 19 (2007): 293–314.

Edlin, Aaron, Andrew Gelman, and Noah Kaplan, "Vote for Charity's Sake," *The Economists' Voice* 5 (2008): 1–4.

Epley, Nicholas and David Dunning, "Feeling 'Holier Than Thou': Are Self-Serving Assessments Produced by Errors in Self- or Social Prediction?" *Journal of Personality and Social Psychology* 79 (2000): 861–875.

Eskeland, Gunnar and Tarhan Feyzioglu, "Rationing Can Backfire: The 'Day without a Car' in Mexico City," *The World Bank Economic Review* 11 (1997): 383–408.

Estés, Clarissa Pinkola, "Letter to a Young Activist During Troubled Times," *Maven Productions*, 2003. Accessed 12.4.19. Available online at: www.mavenproductions.com/letter-to-a-young-activist

Estlund, David, *Democratic Authority*. Princeton: Princeton University Press, 2008.

FairVote, "Voter Turnout." Accessed 5.27.19. Available online at: www.fairvote.org/voter_turnout#voter_turnout_101

Feldman, Fred, "An Examination of Kantian Ethics," in *Moral Philosophy: A Reader*. Indianapolis: Hackett, 2003, 214–228.

Ferejohn, John and Morris Fiorina, "The Paradox of Not Voting: A Decision Theoretic Analysis," *American Political Science Review* 68 (1974): 525–536.

Ferguson, Adam, *An Essay on the History of Civil Society*, 5th ed. London: T. Cadell, 1782. Accessed 6.6.19. Available online at: https://oll.libertyfund.org/titles/1428

Fernbach, Philip, Todd Rogers, Craig Fox, and Steven Sloman, "Political Extremism is Supported by an Illusion of Understanding," *Psychological Science* 24 (2013): 939–946.

First Amendment Center of the Freedom Forum Institute, "The 2018 State of the First Amendment," 2018. Accessed 5.27.2019. Available online at: www.freedomforuminstitute.org/wp-content/uploads/2018/06/2018_FFI_SOFA_Report.pdf

Flynn, D.J., Brendan Nyhan, and Jason Reifler, "The Nature and Origins of Misperceptions: Understanding False and Unsupported Beliefs About Politics." *Advances in Political Psychology* 38 (2017): 127–150.

Foot, Philippa, *Virtues and Vices*. Oxford: Oxford University Press, 2002.

Foot, Philippa, *Natural Goodness*. Oxford: Oxford University Press, 2003.

Franklin, Benjamin, *The Works of Benjamin Franklin*. Jared Sparks, ed. Boston: Hilliard, Gray, and Company, 1836.

Freeder, Sean, Gabriel Lenz, and Shad Turney, "The Importance of Knowing 'What Goes with What': Reinterpreting the Evidence on Policy Attitude Stability," *The Journal of Politics* 81 (2019): 274–290.

Freiman, Christopher, *Unequivocal Justice*. New York: Routledge, 2017.

Frimer, Jeremy, Linda Skitka, and Matt Moytl, "Liberals and Conservatives Are Similarly Motivated to Avoid Exposure to One Another's Opinions," *Journal of Experimental Social Psychology* 72 (2017): 1–12.

Galanes, Philip, "Ruth Bader Ginsburg and Gloria Steinem on the Unending Fight for Women's Rights," *The New York Times* 11.14.15. Accessed 1.5.19. Available online at: www.nytimes.com/2015/11/15/fashion/ruth-bader-ginsburg-and-gloria-steinem-on-the-unending-fight-for-womens-rights.html

Gampa, Anup, Sean Wojcik, Matt Motyl, Brian Nosek, and Peter Ditto, "(Ideo)Logical Reasoning: Ideology Impairs Sound Reasoning," *Social Psychological and Personality Science* (2019). Available online at: https://doi.org/10.1177/1948550619829059

Gelman, Andrew, Gary King, and John Boscardin, "Estimating the Probability of Events that Have Never Occurred: When Is Your Vote Decisive?" *Journal of the American Statistical Association* 93 (1998): 1–9.

Gelman, Andrew, Nate Silver, and Aaron Edlin, "What is the Probability Your Vote Will Make a Difference?" *Economic Inquiry* 50 (2012): 321–326.

Gerber, Alan and Gregory Huber, "Partisanship, Political Control, and Economic Assessments," *American Journal of Political Science* 54 (2010): 153–173.

Gift, Karen and Thomas Gift, "Does Politics Influence Hiring? Evidence from a Randomized Experiment," *Political Behavior* 37 (2015): 653–675.

Why It's OK to Ignore Politics

GiveWell Cost-Effectiveness Analysis—Version 4, 2019. Accessed 6.26.19. Available online at: https://docs.google.com/spreadsheets/d/1_bNbnVaAUQSq4fIzGBU_wVWojmwZrvQKzjSRx92y6wc/edit#gid=1364064522

Givewell.org, "Top Charities." Accessed 6.4.19. Available online at: www.givewell.org/charities/top-charities

Goldman, Alvin, "Why Citizens Should Vote: A Causal Responsibility Approach to Voting," *Social Philosophy and Policy* 16 (1999): 201–217.

Gomberg, Paul, "The Fallacy of Philanthropy," *Canadian Journal of Philosophy* 32 (2002): 29–65.

Gonzales, Nathan, "Are There Really Fewer Competitive House Districts Than Ever Before?" *Roll Call* 9.3.13. Accessed 5.30.19. Available online at: www.rollcall.com/rothenblog/fewer-competitive-house-districts-than-ever-before-not-exactly/

Green, Donald and Ian Shapiro, *Pathologies of Rational Choice Theory*. New Haven: Yale University Press, 1994.

Greene, Joshua, *Moral Tribes: Emotion, Reason, and the Gap Between Us and Them*. New York: Penguin Press, 2013.

Groenendyk, Eric, "Justifying Party Identification: A Case of Identifying with the 'Lesser of Two Evils,'" *Political Behavior* 34 (2012): 453–475.

Groenendyk, Eric, "Competing Motives in a Polarized Electorate: Political Responsiveness, Identity Defensiveness, and the Rise of Partisan Antipathy," *Advances in Political Psychology* 39 (2018): 159–171.

Guerrero, Alexander, "The Paradox of Voting and the Ethics of Political Representation," *Philosophy and Public Affairs* 38 (2010): 272–306.

Guglielmi, Giorgia, Rodrigo Pérez Ortega, T.V. Padma, Holly Else, Quirin Schiermeier, and Barbara Casassus, "The March for Science is Back—and Here's What to Expect," *Nature* 4.12.18. Accessed 5.30.19. Available online at: www.nature.com/articles/d41586-018-04474-w

Gutting, Gary, "Is Voting Out of Self-Interest Wrong?" *The New York Times* 3.31.16. Accessed 6.4.19. Available online at: https://opinionator.blogs.nytimes.com/2016/03/31/is-voting-out-of-self-interest-wrong/

Hanna, Nathan, "An Argument for Voting Abstention," *Public Affairs Quarterly* 23 (2009): 275–286.

Hart, H.L.A., "Are There Any Natural Rights?" *Philosophical Review* 64 (1955): 175–191.

Hart, Kim, "Exclusive Poll: Most Democrats See Republicans as Racist, Sexist," *Axios* 11.12.2018. Accessed 6.17.19. Available online at: www.axios.com/poll-democrats-and-republicans-hate-each-other-racist-ignorant-evil-99ae7afc-5a51-42be-8ee2-3959e43ce320.html

Hastorf, Albert and Hadley Cantril, "They Saw a Game; A Case Study," *The Journal of Abnormal and Social Psychology* 49 (1954): 129–134.

Hetherington, Marc, "Turned Off or Turned On? How Polarization Affects Political Engagement," in Pietro Nivola and David Brady, eds. *Red and Blue Nation? Consequences and Correction of America's Polarized Politics*. Washington, DC: Brookings, 2008, 1–33.

Holmes, Jack, "4 Veterans Share Their True Feelings About the NFL National Anthem Protests," *Esquire* 11.17.17. Accessed 1.5.19. Available online at: www.esquire.com/news-politics/a13788869/4-veterans-nfl-national-anthem-protests/

Hooks, Christopher, "#TBT: How A Philly Cheesesteak Destroyed America," *Vice* 4.26.18. Accessed 6.6.19. Available online at: www.vice.com/en_us/article/3kj9vj/tbt-how-a-philly-cheesesteak-destroyed-america

Horton, Joe, "The All or Nothing Problem," *Journal of Philosophy* 114 (2017): 94–104.

Huddy, Leonie, Stanley Feldman, and Erin Cassese, "On the Distinct Political Effects of Anxiety and Anger," in W. Russell Neuman, George Marcus, Michael MacKuen, and Ann Crigler, eds. *The Affect Effect: Dynamics of Emotion in Political Thinking and Behavior*. Chicago: University of Chicago Press, 2007, 202–230.

Huemer, Michael, "In Praise of Passivity," *Studia Humana* 2 (2012): 12–28.

Huemer, Michael, "Why People are Irrational about Politics," in Jonathan Anomaly, Geoffrey Brennan, Michael Munger, and Geoffrey Sayre-McCord, eds. *Philosophy, Politics, and Economics: An Anthology*. Oxford: Oxford University Press, 2016, 456–467.

Hursthouse, Rosalind, *On Virtue Ethics*. Oxford: Oxford University Press, 1999.

Ingraham, Christopher, "About 100 Million People Couldn't be Bothered to Vote this Year," *Washington Post* 11.12.16. Accessed 7.1.19. Available online at: www.washingtonpost.com/news/wonk/wp/2016/11/12/about-100-million-people-couldnt-be-bothered-to-vote-this-year/

Iyengar, Shanto and Masha Krupenkin, "The Strengthening of Partisan Affect," *Advances in Political Psychology* 39 (2018): 201–218.

Iyengar, Shanto, Yphtach Lelkes, Matthew Levendusky, Neil Malhotra, and Sean Westwood, "The Origins and Consequences of Affective Polarization in the United States" *Annual Review of Political Science* 22 (2019): 129–146.

Iyengar, Shanto, Gaurav Sood, and Yphtach Lelkes, "Affect, Not Ideology: A Social Identity Perspective on Polarization," *Public Opinion Quarterly* 76 (2012): 405–431.

Iyengar, Shanto and Sean Westwood, "Fear and Loathing Across Party Lines: New Evidence on Group Polarization," *American Journal of Political Science* 59 (2015): 690–707.

Joint United Nations Programme on HIV/AIDS, *UNAIDS Outlook Report June 2010.* Geneva, Switzerland: 2010.

Joshi, Hrishikesh, "What are the Chances You're Right About Everything? An Epistemic Challenge for Modern Partisanship," Unpublished Manuscript, 2019.

Kagan, Shelly, *The Limits of Morality.* Oxford: Clarendon Press, 1989.

Kahan, Dan, "Ideology, Motivated Reasoning, and Cognitive Reflection," *Judgment and Decision Making* 8 (2013): 407–424.

Kahan, Dan, "Climate-Science Communication and the Measurement Problem," *Political Psychology* 36 (2015): 1–43.

Kahan, Dan, "The Politically Motivated Reasoning Paradigm, Part 1: What Politically Motivated Reasoning Is and How to Measure It," in R.A. Scott and S.M. Kosslyn, eds. *Emerging Trends in the Social and Behavioral Sciences,* 2016a. doi:10.1002/9781118900772.etrds0417

Kahan, Dan, "The Politically Motivated Reasoning Paradigm, Part 2: Unanswered Questions," in R.A. Scott and S.M. Kosslyn, eds. *Emerging Trends in the Social and Behavioral Sciences,* 2016b. doi:10.1002/9781118900772. etrds0418

Kahan, Dan, Donald Braman, Geoffrey Cohen, John Gastil, and Paul Slovic, "Who Fears the HPV Vaccine, Who Doesn't, and Why? An Experimental Study of the Mechanisms of Cultural Cognition," *Law and Human Behavior* 34 (2010): 501–516.

Kahan, Dan, David Hoffman, Donald Braman, Danieli Evans, and Jeffrey Rachlinski, "They Saw A Protest: Cognitive Illiberalism and the Speech-Conduct Distinction," *Stanford Law Review* 64 (2012): 851–906.

Kahan, Dan, Hank Jenkins-Smith, and Donald Braman, "Cultural Cognition of Scientific Consensus," *Journal of Risk Research* 14 (2011): 147–174.

Kahan, Dan and Ellen Peters, "Rumors of the 'Nonreplication' of the 'Motivated Numeracy Effect' Are Greatly Exaggerated," *Yale Law and Economics Research Paper No. 584* (2017). Available online at: https://dx.doi.org/ 10.2139/ssrn.3026941

Kahan, Dan, Ellen Peters, Erica Cantrell Dawson, and Paul Slovic, "Motivated Numeracy and Enlightened Self-Government," *Behavioural Public Policy* 1 (2017): 54–86.

Kalmoe, Nathan and Lilliana Mason, "Lethal Mass Partisanship: Prevalence, Correlates, and Electoral Contingencies." Prepared for presentation at the January 2019 NCAPSA American Politics Meeting. Unpublished Manuscript 2019.

Kaplan, Jonas, Sarah Gimbel, and Sam Harris, "Neural Correlates of Maintaining One's Political Beliefs in the Face of Counterevidence," *Scientific Reports* 6 (2016): 1–11.

Karnofsky, Holden, "The Lack of Controversy Over Well-Targeted Aid," *The GiveWell Blog* 11.6.15. Accessed 5.30.19. Available online at: https://blog.givewell.org/2015/11/06/the-lack-of-controversy-over-well-targeted-aid/

Kelman, Herbert, "Violence Without Moral Restraint: Reflections on the Dehumanization of Victims and Victimizers," *Journal of Social Issues* 29 (1973): 25–61.

Kleinfeld, Rachel, Richard Youngs, and Jonah Belser, "Renewing U.S. Political Representation: Lessons From Europe and U.S. History," *Carnegie Endowment for International Peace* 3.12.18. Accessed 6.17.19. Available online at: https://carnegieendowment.org/2018/03/12/renewing-u.s.-political-representation-lessons-from-europe-and-u.s-history-pub-75758

Klosko, George, *The Principle of Fairness and Political Obligation.* Savage, MD: Rowman and Littlefield, 1992.

Kteily, Nour, Emile Bruneau, Adam Waytz, and Sarah Cotterill, "The Ascent of Man: Theoretical and Empirical Evidence for Blatant Dehumanization," *Journal of Personality and Social Psychology* 109 (2015): 901–931.

Levendusky, Matthew and Neil Malhotra, "(Mis)perceptions of Partisan Polarization in the American Public," *Public Opinion Quarterly* 80 (2016): 378–391.

Lodge, Milton and Charles Taber, "Three Steps Toward a Theory of Motivated Political Reasoning," in Arthur Lupia, Mathew McCubbins, and Samuel Popkin, eds., *Elements of Reason: Understanding and Expanding the Limits of Political Rationality.* London: Cambridge University Press, 2000, 183–213.

Lomasky, Loren and Geoffrey Brennan, "Is There a Duty to Vote?" *Social Philosophy and Policy* 17 (2000): 62–86.

Long, A.A. and D.N. Sedley, *The Hellenistic Philosophers, Volume 1: Translations of the Principal Sources, with Philosophical Commentary.* Cambridge: Cambridge University Press, 1987.

Lord, Charles, Lee Ross, and Mark Lepper, "Biased Assimilation and Attitude Polarization: Effects of Prior Theories on Subsequently Considered Evidence," *Journal of Personality and Social Psychology* 37 (1979): 2098–2109.

Lupia, Arthur and Matthew McCubbins. *The Democratic Dilemma: Can Citizens Learn What They Need To Know?* Cambridge: Cambridge University Press, 1998.

Luskin, Robert, "From Denial to Extenuation (and Finally Beyond): Political Sophistication and Citizen Performance," in James Kuklinski, ed. *Thinking About Political Psychology.* New York: Cambridge University Press, 2002, 281–305.

MacAskill, William, *Doing Good Better: How Effective Altruism Can Help You Make a Difference.* New York: Penguin, 2015.

MacAskill, William, Benjamin Todd, and Robert Wiblin, "Can You Guess Which Government Programs Work? Most People Can't," *Vox* 8.17.15. Accessed 6.6.19. Available online at: www.vox.com/2015/8/13/9148123/quiz-which-programs-work

MacKuen, Michael, Jennifer Wolak, Luke Keele, and George Marcus, "Civic Engagements: Resolute Partisanship or Reflective Deliberation," *American Journal of Political Science* 54 (2010): 440–458.

Malhotra, Neil and Gregory Huber, "Political Homophily in Social Relationships: Evidence from Online Dating Behavior," *The Journal of Politics* 79 (2017): 269–283.

Marotta, Jenna, "'On the Basis of Sex' Team Explains Why Ruth Bader Ginsburg 'Is Not a Superhero,'" *The Hollywood Reporter* 11.11.18. Accessed 1.5.19. Available online at: www.hollywoodreporter.com/news/basis-sex-team-talks-subject-ruth-bader-ginsburg-1160001

Martherus, James, Andres Martinez, Paul Piff, Alexander Theodoridis, "Party Animals? Extreme Partisan Polarization and Dehumanization," Unpublished Manuscript 2019.

Maskivker, Julia, "Being a Good Samaritan Requires You to Vote," *Political Studies* 66 (2018): 409–424.

Maskivker, Julia, "It's Your Moral Duty To Vote. Here Are 3 Reasons," *Washington Post* 11.2.16. Accessed 5.27.19. Available online at: www.washingtonpost.com/news/monkey-cage/wp/2016/11/02/its-your-moral-duty-to-vote-here-are-3-reasons/?utm_term=.1ed697e96d14

Mason, Lilliana, "'I Disrespectfully Agree': The Differential Effects of Partisan Sorting on Social and Issue Polarization," *American Journal of Political Science* 59 (2015): 128–145.

Mason, Lilliana, "A Cross-Cutting Calm: How Social Sorting Drives Affective Polarization," *Public Opinion Quarterly* 80 (2016): 351–377.

Mason, Lilliana, *Uncivil Agreement: How Politics Became Our Identity*. Chicago: University of Chicago Press, 2018.

McConnell, Christopher, Yotam Margalit, Neil Malhotra, and Matthew Levendusky, "The Economic Consequences of Partisanship in a Polarized Era," *American Journal of Political Science* 62 (2018): 5–18.

McMahan, Jeff, "Philosophical Critiques of Effective Altruism," *The Philosophers' Magazine* 73 (2016): 92–99.

McRaney, David, "The Neuroscience of Changing Your Mind," *You Are Not So Smart* (Podcast: Episode 93) 1.13.17. Accessed 6.18.19. Available online at: https://youarenotsosmart.com/2017/01/13/yanss-093-the-neuroscience-of-changing-your-mind/

Meehl, Paul, "The Selfish Voter Paradox and the Thrown-Away Vote Argument," *American Political Science Review* 71 (1977): 11–30.

Meffert, Michael, Sungeun Chung, Amber Joiner, Leah Waks, and Jennifer Garst, "The Effects of Negativity and Motivated Information Processing During a Political Campaign," *Journal of Communication* 56 (2006): 27–51.

Menand, Louis, "Everybody's An Expert," *The New Yorker* 11.27.05. Accessed 6.7.19. Available online at: www.newyorker.com/magazine/2005/12/05/everybodys-an-expert

Michael Huemer, "In Praise of Passivity," *Studia Humana* 1 (2012): 12–28.

Mill, John Stuart, "The Collected Works of John Stuart Mill, Volume XIX—Essays on Politics and Society Part II," in John Robson, ed. *Introduction by Alexander Brady*. Toronto: University of Toronto Press; London: Routledge and Kegan Paul, 1977. Accessed 7.3.19. Available online at: https://oll.libertyfund.org/titles/234

Millgram, Elijah, "Reasonably Virtuous," in *Ethics Done Right*. New York: Cambridge University Press, 2005, 133–167.

Mueller, Dennis, *Public Choice III*. Cambridge: Cambridge University Press, 2003.

Mulligan, Casey and Charles Hunter, "The Empirical Frequency of a Pivotal Vote," *Public Choice* 116 (2003): 31–54.

Munro, Geoffrey, Julia Zirpoli, Adam Schuman, and Jeff Taulbee, "Third-Party Labels Bias Evaluations of Political Platforms and Candidates," *Basic and Applied Social Psychology* 35 (2013): 151–163.

Mutz, Diana, *Hearing the Other Side: Deliberative Versus Participatory Democracy*. Cambridge: Cambridge University Press, 2006.

Newport, Frank, "Americans Most Confident in Obama on Economy," *Gallup* 4.13.09. Accessed 6.18.19. Available online at: https://news.gallup.com/poll/117415/Americans-Confident-Obama-Economy.aspx

Newport, Frank, "Democrats, Republicans Agree on Four Top Issues For Campaign," 2.1.16. Accessed 6.26.19. Available online at: https://news.gallup.com/poll/188918/democrats-republicans-agree-four-top-issues-campaign.aspx

New York Times Editorial Board, "Vote. That's Just What They Don't Want You To Do," *New York Times* 3.10.18. Accessed 7.1.19. Available online at: www.nytimes.com/2018/03/10/opinion/sunday/go-vote.html

Nisbet, Erik, Kathryn Cooper, and R. Kelly Garrett, "The Partisan Brain: How Dissonant Science Messages Lead Conservatives and Liberals to (Dis)Trust Science," *The ANNALS of the American Academy of Political and Social Science* 658 (2015): 36–66.

Noel, Hans, "Ten Things Political Scientists Know that You Don't," *The Forum* 8 (2010). doi:10.2202/1540-8884.1393

Noyes, Kolb, "Can't Get Elected Dogcatcher? Try Running In Duxbury, Vt," *National Public Radio* 3.24.18. Accessed 5.30.19. Available online at: www.npr.org/2018/03/24/595755604/cant-get-elected-dogcatcher-try-running-in-duxbury-vt

Nyhan, Brendan and Jason Reifler, "When Corrections Fail: The Persistence of Political Misperceptions," *Political Behavior* 32 (2010): 303–330.

Nyhan, Brendan and Jason Reifler, "The Roles of Information Deficits and Identity Threat in the Prevalence of Misperceptions," *Journal of Elections, Public Opinion and Parties* 29 (2019): 222–244.

Olson, Mancur, *The Logic of Collective Action*. Cambridge, MA: Harvard University Press, 1971.

Owen, Guillermo and Bernard Grofman, "To Vote or Not to Vote: The Paradox of Nonvoting," *Public Choice* 42 (1984): 311–325.

Parfit, Derek, *Reasons and Persons*. Oxford: Oxford University Press, 1984.

Perkins, David, Michael Farady, and Barbara Bushey, "Everyday Reasoning and the Roots of Intelligence," in James Voss, David Perkins, and Judith Segal, eds. *Informal Reasoning and Education*. New York: Routledge, 1991, 83–105.

Petrosino, Anthony, Carolyn Turpin-Petrosino, Meghan Hollis-Peel, and Julia Lavenberg, "'Scared Straight' and Other Juvenile Awareness Programs for Preventing Juvenile Delinquency," *Cochrane Database of Systematic Reviews* (2013): 1–44.

Pew Research Center, "Continued Partisan Divides in Views of the Impact of Free Trade Agreements," 4.24.17. Accessed 6.18.19. Available online at: www.pewresearch.org/fact-tank/2017/04/25/support-for-free-trade-agreements-rebounds-modestly-but-wide-partisan-differences-remain/ft_17-04-24_freetrade_usviews_2/

Pew Research Center, "Elaborating on the Views of AAAS Scientists, Issue by Issue," 7.23.15. Accessed 6.25.19. Available online at: www.pewresearch.org/science/2015/07/23/elaborating-on-the-views-of-aaas-scientists-issue-by-issue/

Pew Research Center, "Partisanship and Political Engagement," 10.24.17. Accessed 5.27.19. Available online at: www.people-press.org/2017/10/24/1-partisanship-and-political-engagement/

Pew Research Center, "Section 3: Political Polarization and Personal Life," 6.12.14a. Accessed 6.17.19. Available online at: www.people-press.org/2014/06/12/section-3-political-polarization-and-personal-life/

Pew Research Center, "Section 5: Political Engagement and Activism," 6.12.14b. Accessed 6.17.19. Available online at: www.people-press.org/2014/06/12/section-5-political-engagement-and-activism/

Pew Research Center, "Trends in Political Values and Core Attitudes: 1987–2007," 3.22.07. Accessed 7.1.19. Available online at: www.pewresearch.org/wp-content/uploads/sites/4/legacy-pdf/312.pdf

Philips, Amber, "Congress's Long History of Inaction on Climate Change, in 6 Acts," *Washington Post* 12.1.15. Accessed 6.25.19. Available online at:

www.washingtonpost.com/news/the-fix/wp/2015/12/01/congresss-long-history-of-inaction-on-climate-change-in-6-parts/?utm_term=.66aaa8c8b1ed

PhilPapers.org, "Abortion." Accessed 6.6.19. Available online at: https://philpapers.org/browse/abortion

Pincione, Guido and Fernando Tesón, *Rational Choice and Democratic Deliberation: A Theory of Discourse Failure.* Cambridge: Cambridge University Press, 2006.

Pinto, Sergio, Panka Bencsik, Tuugi Chuluun, and Carol Graham, "Presidential Elections, Divided Politics, and Happiness in the US," *Human Capital and Economic Development Working Paper Series* 2019. Accessed 6.17.19. Available online at: https://econresearch.uchicago.edu/sites/econresearch.uchicago.edu/files/Pinto_Bencsik_Chuluun_etal_2019_presidential-elections-happiness-us.pdf

Plumer, Brad, "U.S. Carbon Emissions Surged in 2018 Even As Coal Plants Closed," *The New York Times* 1.8.19. Accessed 6.25.19. Available online at: www.nytimes.com/2019/01/08/climate/greenhouse-gas-emissions-increase.html

Politifact, "Tracking Politicians' Promises." Accessed 7.8.19. Available online at: www.politifact.com/truth-o-meter/promises/

Pope Paul VI, "Pastoral Constitution on the Church in the Modern World," 12.7.65. Accessed 7.3.19. Available online at: www.vatican.va/archive/hist_councils/ii_vatican_council/documents/vat-ii_cons_19651207_gaudium-et-spes_en.html

Popkin, Samuel, *The Reasoning Voter. Communication and Persuasion in Presidential Campaigns.* Chicago: University of Chicago Press, 1991.

Prior, Markus, Gaurav Sood, and Kabir Khanna, "You Cannot Be Serious: The Impact of Accuracy Incentives on Partisan Bias in Reports of Economic Perceptions," *Quarterly Journal of Political Science* 10 (2015): 489–518.

Pronin, Emily, Daniel Lin, and Lee Ross, "The Bias Blind Spot: Perceptions of Bias in Self Versus Others," *Personality and Social Psychology Bulletin* 28 (2002): 369–381.

Pronin, Emily, Carolyn Puccio, and Lee Ross, "Understanding Misunderstanding: Social Psychological Perspectives," in Thomas Gilovich, Dale Griffin, and Daniel Kahneman, eds. *Heuristics and Biases: The Psychology of Intuitive Judgment.* New York: Cambridge University Press, 2002, 636–665.

Pummer, Theron, "Whether and Where to Give," *Philosophy and Public Affairs* 44 (2016): 77–95.

Rasmussen Reports, "Toplines—Cap & Trade I—May 7–8, 2009," 5.7.09. Accessed 6.6.19. Available online at: www.rasmussenreports.com/public_content/politics/questions/pt_survey_questions/may_2009/toplines_cap_trade_i_may_7_8_2009

Rawls, John, "Legal Obligation and the Duty of Fair Play," in Sidney Hook, ed. *Law and Philosophy*. New York: New York University Press, 1964, 3–18.

Rawls, John, *A Theory of Justice*, revised ed. Cambridge, MA: Belknap Press of Harvard University Press, 1999.

Redlawsk, David, "Hot Cognition or Cool Consideration?" *Journal of Politics* 64 (2002): 1021–1044.

Reimer, Alex, "Colin Kaepernick's Failure to Vote Tarnishes his Credibility as a Social Activist," *Forbes* 11.10.16. Accessed 7.1.19. Available online at: www.forbes.com/sites/alexreimer/2016/11/10/colin-kaepernicks-failure-to-vote-tarnishes-his-credibility-as-a-social-activist/#45a6f63d4c00

Reuters, "Data Dive: The Emotional Cost of the 2016 Election," 2.7.17. Accessed 6.17.19. Available online at: www.reuters.com/article/us-datadive-election/data-dive-the-emotional-cost-of-the-2016-election-idUSKBN15M1YC

Ridester's 2018 Independent Driver Earnings Survey, 2018. Accessed 1.2.19. Available online at: www.ridester.com/2018-survey/

Riker, William and Peter Ordeshook, "A Theory of the Calculus of Voting," *American Political Science Review* 62 (1968): 25–42.

Robson, David, "The '3.5% Rule': How a Small Minority Can Change the World," *BBC Future* 5.14.19. Accessed 7.2.19. Available online at: www.bbc.com/future/story/20190513-it-only-takes-35-of-people-to-change-the-world

Romer, Paul, "Economic Growth," in David Henderson, ed. *The Concise Encyclopedia of Economics*. Indianapolis: Liberty Fund, 2008, 128–131.

Rozenblit, Leonid, and Frank Keil, "The Misunderstood Limits of Folk Science: An Illusion of Explanatory Depth," *Cognitive Science* 26 (2002): 521–562.

Russell, Bertrand, *Human Knowledge: Its Scope and Limits*. London: Routledge, 2009.

Schkade, David, Cass Sunstein, and Reid Hastie, "What Happened on Deliberation Day?" *California Law Review* 95 (2007): 915–940.

Schmidtz, David, *Elements of Justice*. Cambridge: Cambridge University Press, 2006.

Schwitzgebel, Eric and Joshua Rust, "Do Ethicists and Political Philosophers Vote More Often than Other Professors?" *Review of Philosophy and Psychology* 1 (2010): 189–199.

Shachar, Ron and Barry Nalebuff, "Follow The Leader: Theory and Evidence on Political Participation," *American Economic Review* 89 (1999): 525–547.

Sherman, David and Geoffrey Cohen, "The Psychology of Self-Defense: Self-Affirmation Theory," in Mark Zanna, ed. *Advances in Experimental Social Psychology*, Vol. 38. San Diego, CA: Academic Press, 2006, 183–242.

Shklar, Judith, *Faces of Injustice*. New Haven: Yale University Press, 1990.

Sinclair, Thomas, "Are We Conditionally Obligated to be Effective Altruists?" *Philosophy and Public Affairs* 46 (2018): 36–59.

Singer, Peter, "Famine, Affluence, and Morality," *Philosophy and Public Affairs* 1 (1972): 229–243.

Singer, Peter, *The Life You Can Save*. New York: Random House, 2009.

Singer, Peter, *The Most Good You Can Do*. New Haven: Yale University Press, 2015.

Smith, Adam, *An Inquiry into the Nature and Causes of the Wealth of Nations*. New York: Bantam, 2003.

Smith, Kevin, Matthew Hibbing, and John Hibbing, "Friends, Relatives, Sanity, and Health: The Costs of Politics," *PLoSONE* 14 (2019): 1–13. Available online at: https://doi.org/10.1371/journal.pone.0221870

Somin, Ilya, *Democracy and Political Ignorance*. Stanford: Stanford University Press, 2013.

Somin, Ilya, "The Ongoing Debate Over Political Ignorance: Reply to My Critics," *Critical Review* 27 (2015): 380–414.

Soroka, Stuart and Stephen McAdams, "News, Politics, and Negativity," *Political Communication* 32 (2015): 1–22.

Sparks, Paul, Donna Jessop, James Chapman, and Katherine Holmes, "Pro-Environmental Actions, Climate Change, and Defensiveness: Do Self-Affirmations Make a Difference to People's Motives and Beliefs About Making a Difference?" *British Journal of Social Psychology* 49 (2010): 553–568.

Srinivasan, Amia, "Stop the Robot Apocalypse. Review of *Doing Good Better: Effective Altruism and a Radical New Way to Make a Difference* by William MacAskill," *London Review of Books* (Online) 37 (2015): 3–6. Accessed 5.30.19. Available online at: www.lrb.co.uk/v37/n18/amia-srinivasan/stop-the-robot-apocalypse

Stern, Todd, *The Paris Agreement and Its Future*. Washington DC: Brookings, 2018. Accessed 6.25.19. Available online at: www.brookings.edu/wp-content/uploads/2018/10/The-Paris-Agreement-and-Its-Future-Todd-Stern-October-2018.pdf

Stuart Mill, John, "The Collected Works of John Stuart Mill, Volume XIX—Essays on Politics and Society Part II," in John Robson, ed. *Introduction by Alexander Brady*. Toronto: University of Toronto Press; London: Routledge and Kegan Paul, 1977.

Sturgis, Patrick, "Knowledge and Collective Preferences: A Comparison of Two Approaches to Estimating the Opinions of a Better Informed Public," *Sociological Methods and Research* 31 (2003): 453–485.

Taber, Charles and Milton Lodge, "Motivated Skepticism in the Evaluation of Political Beliefs," *American Journal of Political Science* 50 (2006): 755–769.

Tea, Kristen, "To My Friends Who Are Sick of Politics," 8.15.17. Accessed 1.21.19. Available online at: https://motherwiselife.org/to-my-friends-who-are-sick-of-politics/

Tetlock, Philip, *Expert Political Judgment*. Princeton: Princeton University Press, 2005.

Tetlock, Philip and Dan Gardner, *Superforecasting: The Art and Science of Prediction*. New York: Broadway Books, 2015.

Trading Economics, "United States Average Hourly Wages," 2018. Accessed 1.2.19. Available online at: https://tradingeconomics.com/united-states/wages

U.S. Citizenship and Immigration Services, "Citizenship Rights and Responsibilities." Accessed 7.3.19. Available online at: www.uscis.gov/citizenship/learners/citizenship-rights-and-responsibilities

Valentino, Nicholas, Ted Brader, Eric Groenendyk, Krysha Gregorowicz, and Vincent Hutchings, "Election Night's Alright for Fighting: The Role of Emotions in Political Participation," *The Journal of Politics* 73 (2011): 156–170.

Van Bavel, Jay and Andrea Pereira, "The Partisan Brain: An Identity-Based Model of Political Belief," *Trends in Cognitive Sciences* 22 (2018): 213–224.

Verkuyten, Maykel and Mieke Maliepaard, "A Further Test of the 'Party Over Policy' Effect: Political Leadership and Ethnic Minority Policies," *Basic and Applied Social Psychology* 35 (2013): 241–248.

Wagoner, Nick, "Colin Kaepernick on not Voting: 'There's More than one Way to Create Change,'" *ESPN*. Accessed 12.11.19. Available online at: www.espn.com/nfl/story/_/id/18058256/colin-kaepernick-san-francisco-49ers-not-voting-there-more-one-way-create-change

Waldron, Jeremy, "Participation: The Right of Rights," *Proceedings of the Aristotelian Society* 98 (1998): 307–337.

Weeks, Brian, "Emotions, Partisanship, and Misperceptions: How Anger and Anxiety Moderate the Effect of Partisan Bias on Susceptibility to Political Misinformation," *Journal of Communication* 65 (2015): 699–719.

West, Richard, Russell Meserve, and Keith Stanovich, "Cognitive Sophistication Does Not Attenuate the Bias Blind Spot," *Journal of Personality and Social Psychology* 103 (2012): 506–519.

Westen, Drew, Pavel Blagov, Keith Harenski, and Stephan Hamann, "Neural Bases of Motivated Reasoning: An fMRI Study of Emotional Constraints on Partisan Political Judgment in the 2004 U.S. Presidential Election," *Journal of Cognitive Neuroscience* 18 (2006): 1947–1958.

Westfall, Jacob, Leaf Van Boven, John Chambers, and Charles Judd, "Perceiving Political Polarization in the United States Party Identity Strength and Attitude Extremity Exacerbate the Perceived Partisan Divide," *Perspectives on Psychological Science* 10 (2015): 145–158.

Winerman, Lea, "By the Numbers: Our Stressed-Out Nation," *American Psychological Association*, Monitor on Psychology 48 (2017). Accessed 6.20.19. Available online at: www.apa.org/monitor/2017/12/numbers

Zhu, Jiafeng, "Fairness, Political Obligation, and the Justificatory Gap," *Journal of Moral Philosophy* 12 (2015): 290–312.